MW01199457

"Nuanced, huma. , cally literate, this is a wonderful contribution to Christian reflection both within and beyond the Orthodox Church. It is not some indiscriminate plea for Enlightenment ethics to take over from theology, but a fresh, careful sifting and highlighting of the tradition itself, manifestly seeking the integrity and spiritual health of the Body of Christ."
—ROWAN WILLIAMS, former archbishop of Canterbury

"Carrie Frederick Frost makes a dire claim: the Orthodox Church is already in a state of schism over women. But Frost also knows that God excels in reconciling the estranged. In this brief, beautiful study, Frost courageously names where Orthodox practice has betrayed the gospel, proposes solutions of theological and spiritual integrity, and envisions a Church that any woman, of any tradition, would be pleased and proud for her granddaughter to call home."
—SARAH HINLICKY WILSON, author of *Woman, Women, and the Priesthood in the Trinitarian Theology of Elisabeth Behr-Sigel*

"A thoughtfully compiled and deeply personal contemplation on the complexity of being a practicing Orthodox Christian woman today. This book is a helpful tool for both men and women navigating their personal and spiritual path within the complexity of Orthodoxy with its incredible theology and its distinct cultural heritage bearing a lingering problematic of twenty centuries of patriarchal legacy."
—ELENA NARINSKAYA, co-editor of *Women and Ordination in the Orthodox Church*

"Carrie Frederick Frost's excellent review of the ways Eastern and Oriental Orthodox Churches can move to a revitalized future brings encouragement to all who recognize the resurrection in every living person. Her careful review of customs regarding women is rooted in the gospel teachings of the dignity and value of all. *Church of Our Granddaughters* is required reading for anyone who hopes the tradition of women deacons can be recovered throughout all Christianity."

—PHYLLIS ZAGANO, Hofstra University

"Carrie Frederick Frost's work is convicting and compelling, heartbreaking and heartening. To read it is to hear a prophetic voice, fueled by *agape*, calling the Orthodox Church to repentance. Blending incisive arguments, historical evidence, and personal experiences, *Church of Our Granddaughters* invites readers to restore and release the vibrancy of Orthodoxy's tradition on pastoral care for women and female leadership and ministry. It should be read by every hierarch, priest, deacon, and lay person who cares about Orthodox Christianity's present—and future."

—PERRY T. HAMALIS, North Central College

"Carrie Frederick Frost offers a breath of fresh air in tackling the role of women in the Orthodox Church. She is honest and courageous in confronting both the challenges that still face women, and positive in providing constructive ways forward. Issues of 'purity,' equality, and leadership affect every member of the Church regardless of their gender. Frost is balanced and scholarly, but also passionate in her drive to bring about change for future generations."

—MARY B. CUNNINGHAM, University of Nottingham

# Church of Our
# Granddaughters

# Church of Our Granddaughters

CARRIE FREDERICK FROST

*Foreword by Vigen Guroian*

CASCADE *Books* · Eugene, Oregon

CHURCH OF OUR GRANDDAUGHTERS

Cascade Books
An Imprint of Wipf and Stock Publishers
199 W. 8th Ave., Suite 3
Eugene, OR 97401

www.wipfandstock.com

PAPERBACK ISBN: 978-1-6667-4485-9
HARDCOVER ISBN: 978-1-6667-4486-6
EBOOK ISBN: 978-1-6667-4487-3

*Cataloguing-in-Publication data:*

Names: Frost, Carrie Frederick [author]. | Guroian, Vigen [foreword writer].

Title: Church of our granddaughters / by Carrie Frederick Frost.

Description: Eugene, OR: Cascade Books, 2023 | Includes bibliographical references and index.

Identifiers: ISBN 978-1-6667-4485-9 (paperback) | ISBN 978-1-6667-4486-6 (hardcover) | ISBN 978-1-6667-4487-3 (ebook)

Subjects: LCSH: Women in the Orthodox Eastern Church. | Christian women—Religious life. | Ordination of women—Orthodox Eastern Church. | Women in church work—Orthodox Eastern Church. | Women—Religious aspects—Christianity.

Classification: BX341.52 F76 2023 (paperback) | BX341.52 (ebook)

02/19/23

*For our granddaughters*

# Contents

# Foreword

Carrie Frederick Frost begins this book with a story. There is real life grit in it. Like sandpaper on the skin, I can feel it. As an Orthodox Christian I have been in conversations akin to the one Frost recounts. But the fact that I am a man and not a woman makes me extra cautious about addressing, as she does, the role of women in the church and the obstacles that exist to their fullest participation in it. What do I know?

Frost tells us of an encounter that happened in a reading group in which her book, *Maternal Body: An Incarnational Theology from the Christian East*, was being discussed. One of the women participants asked how Frost could tolerate the status of women in the Orthodox Church. The woman, who was not herself Orthodox, said, "I don't like the absence of women priests in Orthodoxy and the treatment of women in the Orthodox Church. Why would you stay?"

Frost wasn't defensive, though she could have been. Neither did she take the bait of a strong dose of individualist and voluntarist bias in the person's question. Rather, she spoke as one might expect an Orthodox Christian would do. She made it clear that she felt she belonged to a real community in which love abides. She answered that she "grew up surrounded by pious and inspiring Orthodox Christian women and men," adding: "There is much that sustains me in the Orthodox Church." Nonetheless, Frost tells us, the conversation has stayed with her. "There was truth in it because the Orthodox Church does fail 'to honor and meet the needs of . . . women.'"

It is well that Carrie Frederick Frost begins *Church of Our Granddaughters* this way. It helps us to understand that however

critical she may be of insensitive and, yes, even misogynist behav-
iors and practices in the Orthodox Church, her call for reform
remains respectful of the lived truth of the Orthodox faith. She remains a loyal daughter of the Church and seeks reform from within
it, attentive to the grain of the Church's history and tradition. Clear
evidence for this is the manner in which she handles the question of
women in the priesthood. Whilst the inquirer in her story harshly
criticizes the Orthodox Church for the exclusion of women in the
priesthood, Frost is respectful of the fact that this exclusion is a
long and uninterrupted part of tradition. However, she also insists
that a living tradition ought to be open to a conversation about the
matter. Her position is different in her support for the reinstitution
of the office of deaconess in the Church. This is because the office
of deaconess has existed in the Church's history, and for not a brief
time at that. Were this office of the deaconess to be reinstituted, she
argues, then a conversation about women in the priesthood might
be even more warranted than at present; though she is clear that the
status of deacon or deaconess does not logically or necessarily lead
to the priesthood. The path from deaconess to priest remains only a
possibility under "the guidance of the Holy Spirit."

I now would like to tell a story of my own. If this adds some
small measure of levity to the discussion, then that surely is a help.
I, however, also believe that my story adds a measure of hope that
the Orthodox Church (or is it Orthodox people we are speaking
of here) is awakening to the kind of re-envisioning of the Church
for which Frost pleads. The event happened some forty-five years
ago. Because there was not an Armenian church near where June
and I and our firstborn child, Rafi, were living, I would often attend a Greek Orthodox church. Among those I knew in the parish
was a university colleague who was at that time the chair of the
parish council. The day was a special day in the Orthodox tradition. It was the Holy Feast of Orthodoxy that celebrates the defeat
of iconoclasm and the restitution of icons in the churches. There is
procession in the service that circles the sanctuary with of all the
icons in the church held high by the participants.

Just moments before the procession was to begin, my colleague
hurried up to the pew in which I was seated, and whispered, "Vigen,

we need your help. I need you to carry one of the icons in the procession." I whispered in reply, "How is that possible? You know very well that I am not even permitted to take communion here." The Armenian Church, among several other Orthodox Churches, such as the Coptic Church and the Syriac Orthodox Church of Antioch, do not accept the two nature's Christological formula (or creed) of the fourth of Ecumenical Council of Chalcedon in 451, though they affirm that Christ is wholly God and wholly human. Called the Oriental Orthodox Churches, these Churches are not in communion with the greater Eastern Orthodox Church. My colleague then said: "No matter. We have run out of men to carry the icons. Women are not allowed." So I obliged. As I looked onto the pews and saw that we were circling only women and children, I had to laugh to myself at the absurdity of it all.

Over the years, I have told this story many times when it fits the occasion, and that usually is about the status of women in the Orthodox Churches, Eastern and Oriental. Then about a dozen years ago, I attended the same Greek Orthodox church, again on Orthodox Sunday. This time, mercifully, I was not asked to participate in the procession of icons. Rather the icons were carried by the children of the church, boys and girls alike.

What happened? What made the difference? How did the prohibition against women in the procession disappear? Was there in fact an official dictum to that effect or was this a fiat of the parish priest? I never asked. None of that is as important as what I witnessed with my own eyes.

I leave my story to stand on its own. I don't believe there is much need for interpretation. My story does not, in and of itself, prove that the Orthodox Church has turned the curve on the place of women in the Orthodox Church. Though I believe it is a hopeful sign along the way.

*Church of Our Granddaughters* is also a hopeful sign. It is a one-off, for I do not know of anything like it for its subject matter, elegance, theological depth, passion, or readability. It is an exceptionally good book!

Vigen Guroian
Culpeper, Virginia
The Feast of the Exaltation of the Cross, September 2022

# Acknowledgments

Thank you to those friends, relations, and colleagues who read drafts of some, or all, of this book: Patricia Fann Bouteneff, Peter Bouteneff, Father John Chryssavgis, Father Marc Dunaway, Matt Frost, Vigen Guroian, Agnes Howard, Ann Marie Mecera, Presbytera Elizabeth Tervo, Helen Theodoropoulos, Marilyn Rouvelas, and Reverend Sarah Hinlicky Wilson. I am forever grateful for your feedback. Special thanks to the entire Dunaway family, whose hospitality and willingness to hash things through opened up new ways of thinking for me.

Thank you to my family—living and dead; at home and away—for your formative love and support. I am grateful for my parents, Eustace and Menodora (Frankie); may their memories be eternal. Thank you to my wonderful husband and love of my life, Matt. And I give my love and appreciation for our children and our daughter-in-law: Cyrus and Svetlana, Annie, Eliza, Beatrix, and Ignatius.

When I began writing this book, grandchildren of my own were purely speculative. But the joyous announcement of an expected grandchild came as I completed the manuscript, bringing the title and hopes for the book even closer to my heart.

# Introduction

## WOMEN IN THE ORTHODOX
## CHURCH TODAY

*"How can you stand it?"* asked my interlocutor, with a certain amount of vim, possibly venom, in reference to my being both a woman and an Orthodox Christian.

This person was also a woman but not an Orthodox Christian; she belonged to a church that has included women in positions of leadership, including its priesthood, for decades. She was part of a book group reading a book of mine—*Maternal Body: An incarnational Theology from the Christian East*—that addresses the ways that the Orthodox Church falls short in ministering to its mothers (and, by extension, women and men more broadly). Hers was one of the first questions of the evening. I asked her to explain what she meant. She said, "I don't like the absence of women priests in Orthodoxy and the treatment of women in the Orthodox Church. Why would you stay? The Orthodox Church clearly has a woman problem."

I took a deep breath and explained what I have explained many times to people inside and outside the Orthodox Church and, frankly, to myself as well. I *can* stand it—in fact, I can more than stand it—I *love* the Orthodox Church. I grew up surrounded by pious and inspiring Orthodox Christian women and men. My father's parents came to the United States from Belarus and Ukraine bringing their Orthodoxy with them to southern West

Virginia. My mother converted to Orthodoxy. I was baptized and married in the same church in which my family members were baptized and married. I was immersed in the liturgy from an early age; some of my earliest and most comforting memories are the smell of incense and taste of the Eucharist. I love the cloud of witnesses of saints and their testimony to the many ways it is possible to live a good Christian life. I understand the Orthodox Church to be the home of the living and triune God, through its lineage back to Jesus Christ and the apostles. There is so much that sustains me in the Orthodox Church.

Still, though, her question stayed with me: *How can you stand it?* It stayed with me because it is a legitimate question. It stayed with me because many Orthodox women and men, in reaction to the Orthodox Church's current place for women—and I am by no means referring only to the absence of women from the ordained clergy—decide, in fact, that they cannot stand it, and they leave. The question stayed with me because I worry that my own daughters and my own sons will decide they cannot stand it. When I am honest with myself, I have times when I wonder if I can continue to stand it.

The question lingered because it forced me to grapple with two realities. First, the fact that Orthodox Church currently fails to honor and meet the needs of its women every day. Second, and at the same time, the real possibility that the Orthodox Church could begin to live out its teachings more adequately and bring about healing change for women, providing dignity, succor, support, and sustenance, so that no one need ask or wonder: *How can you stand it?*

The allegation that the Orthodox Church has a "woman problem" also lingered with me. Does the Orthodox Church have a woman problem? I offer examples that illustrate some realities of women's lives in the Orthodox Church today.

- A teenage girl is excommunicated from the Eucharist during her period, even though she has been to confession and otherwise faithfully prepared. Instead, she watches her brothers go to the chalice without her.

- A woman miscarries a pregnancy, and the Prayers for Miscarriage available to most priests conflate miscarriage with abortion. She hears from her priest's lips that she is to blame for the loss of her pregnancy.

- A mother returning to church for the first time after giving birth is told in the Churching prayers that she is impure, defiled, and unclean from the act of childbirth.

- In the Covid-19 era, most streamed services showed only men—priests, readers, deacons, chanters, etc.—making it easy to imagine that women are invisible and entirely inessential to the Orthodox Church.

- Councils and synods of bishops convene to discuss issues regarding women's lives—inter-Christian and inter-faith marriage, divorce, suicide, contraception, etc.—and women are rarely present or involved in a meaningful way.

- Women experience major life-events—marriage, divorce, pregnancy, miscarriage, menarche, illness, spiritual crises—without the church-sanctioned spiritual guidance and leadership of other women. Because all major clergy and nearly all minor clergy are men in the Orthodox Church, women suffer from the lack of women in clerical ministry.

From these examples, a "woman problem" in the Orthodox Church is well-illustrated. Just because the Orthodox Church has positive connotations with "patriarchs" in an ecclesial sense (the lead bishops), this does not preclude describing the Orthodox Church as *patriarchal* in the contemporary, descriptive sense of the word. We should not be tentative or afraid of calling it as it is: women have been far too often diminished, degraded, and disenfranchised in the Orthodox Church because of its patriarchal ethos.

Yet, all this takes place within the church of Jesus Christ, who included women among his closest friends and who appeared to them after the Resurrection and who radically affirmed women's parity with men. The early church—even within larger cultural constraints—heeded this call in many ways, including affirming the leadership of women in house churches. The ordained order of deaconesses served communities liturgically and pastorally. The Christological orientation of the Orthodox Church sees women and men as *both* made in the image and likeness of God and *both* called to deification. As scholar Pauline Kollonati states, "In Orthodox teaching, men and women are equal before God and they share a common humanity. This would appear to be the perfect basis on which to promote the fullest participation of women in all areas of the ministry."[1]

The institutional Orthodox Church has never fully realized this ideal. We cannot say we were not forewarned; oppressive structures toward women are part of the fallen world (Gen 3:16), at least in the context of marriage: "[your husband] shall rule over you." The bottom line is simple: Orthodox Christian theology in its fullness affirms the humanity and dignity of women, but its practices, teachings, and structures fall short.

However, we don't just live after the Fall, we live in *anno domini*; we live after the Incarnation of Jesus Christ. This changes everything. It changes the way we should approach the Orthodox Church's woman problem. Our ministry is not to complacently accept the brokenness of our reality and continue to impose pre-existing oppressive conditions, but instead to work as well as we can, this side of the kingdom, to perfect and transfigure the world, including the Orthodox Church itself. We must evaluate when and where it has failed to live up to its own principles and swiftly work to remedy those situations so that Orthodox women are valued as much as men throughout their lifetimes, from womb to grave.

We must affirm the value of the "incarnational realities" of women. The Orthodox Church teaches the essential, equally shared humanity of women and men, but there is no sense that this *equality* means perfect equivalency. Instead, it appreciates the ways the human experience is lived out differently between women and men, acknowledging that the "incarnational realties" of women and men are not the same. (I will elaborate on "incarnational realities" in chapter 1.)

---

1. Kollontai, "Contemporary Thinking," 176.

Today, the Orthodox Church is in a time of change concerning women, a time of promise and possibility. I offer another series of examples of Orthodox women's lives today.

- The theologically and pastorally indefensible practices that prohibit girls and women from receiving the Eucharist during menstruation are being proclaimed as incompatible with the doctrine and theology of the Orthodox Church by many priests, hierarchs, synods, theologians, and laypeople.

- The prayers for both miscarriage and Churching are being revised in many parts of the Orthodox world so that they are theologically correct and pastorally comforting in the case of miscarriage and appropriately welcoming in the case of Churching.

- Despite what was shown in Covid live-streaming liturgies, women are increasingly participating in the liturgical life of the Orthodox Church as readers, chanters, choir members and directors, hymnographers, and iconographers.

- Women are included in leadership roles of the Orthodox Church in ways unimaginable even a generation ago: as chief financial officers of jurisdictions, on parish and metropolitan councils, as officers and members of seminary boards, and as seminary professors. Women are also entering church-related fields in greater numbers than ever before: as iconographers, historians, ecclesiastical tailors, hymnographers, chanters, readers, chancery officials, theologians, historians, and so forth.

- In terms of ordained ministry, many calls from different parts of the Orthodox world to reinstitute the order of deaconesses have been issued, and the Patriarchate of Alexandria, the Orthodox Church in Africa, consecrated deaconesses over the last several years.

The vast, unprecedented, and ongoing change of women's roles and engagement today is another way to answer the question of a women problem. Orthodox Christian women continue to exercise their own agency—limited though it may be—to create and sustain lives of meaning.[2] As women enter these new aspects of church life and leadership, the consequences are and will be far reaching. There is no going back. The Orthodox Church is beginning to live out its teachings more fully.

There is a third way to answer the question, which is to say that it is the wrong question. Even the phrase "woman problem" carries a sort of insinuation of being out of step with contemporary norms. This ought not be a concern. Contemporary norms may reasonably prompt conversation within the Orthodox Church, but it is the Church's own premises and standards that are relevant and at stake. It is more appropriate therefore to ask: does the Orthodox Church have a "human" problem that is seen when we consider the position of women in the Orthodox Church today?

Many, if not all, of the "woman problems" in the Orthodox Church are—one way or another—about the subjugation of women relating to their bodies: about the mistaken, theologically insupportable, and pastorally harmful idea that women are, or can be at times, spiritually and physically impure or unclean because of the physical processes of menstruation and lochia (bleeding after childbirth). This "othering" of women, this distancing from their shared common humanity with men, comes from and has perpetuated views of women as inferior. These views have been institutionalized in the Orthodox Church's practices.

The Incarnation, however, cast the Christian understanding of impurity into categories of sin and matters of the will, not bodily circumstance. This is of utmost importance to Orthodox Christians because our understanding of the body is deeply involved in the way we know Jesus Christ. Many of the heretical ideas around Jesus in the early church inflated his divinity at the price of his humanity because it was so hard to accept that God would take on a human body in all of its messiness and squalor. Indeed, this messiness, all this flesh and blood, is why the early Christian theologian Irenaeus called the Incarnation a scandal.

We embrace and celebrate the human body in light of the Incarnation, not as an idol to worship and not because we are gods,

2. For many such examples, see Merdjanova, *Women and Religiosity*.

but because, to reference the patristic maxim, God became human so that we might become like God. Our bodies are blessed by the Incarnation as the workshop for the transfiguration and deification of our whole person. When women's bodies are set aside as impure, unclean, or defiled, we fail to honor the reality and truth of Jesus Christ's Incarnation. We potentially compromise our own transfiguration and deification—not just for women, but for the entire community.

Nothing that might be labeled a "woman problem" in the Orthodox Church is just about women. These so-called women's issues are *cosmic* issues. They are far-reaching, they have pastoral and theological consequences for all of us— women, men, and children of all ages. My best answer to the "women problem" question is that the Orthodox Church has a systematic and universal problem. The oppressive structures of the Orthodox Church are oppressive *in relation to Orthodox doctrine*, not according to any pressures from the secular world to conform to a certain model of equality. In the words of Elisabeth Behr-Sigel, the church has shared a "conviction about the fundamental equality of men and women and their common deification," but this is "a talent that Christians have often hidden under the ground and that others, not of the church (or at least not considering themselves of the church) have sometimes better developed and made more fruitful than Christians themselves."[3]

The Orthodox Church has solutions for this cosmic problem. One of them is specifically a "woman solution," if you will: the process of bringing church practices around women into alignment with theology will free the entire Orthodox Church from oppressive notions about the human body and allow women to enter new roles. This has the dual effect of bringing real and positive change to women within the Orthodox Church and strengthening its incarnational witness to the world at a time when this witness is sorely needed. Also, the Orthodox Church, which has been so masculine in structure and theology, will benefit from an infusion of the feminine.[4]

---

3. Behr-Sigel, *Ministry of Women*, 91.
4. Louth, review of *All Shall Be Saved*, 235.

There is much work to be done by the whole Orthodox Church. All of us who care about the overall health of the church ought to engage in it. This work is too important to be left to left only to women, or to the clergy, or delegated to the laity. This work needs to be done by *all* of us because it is for the good of the whole community. As Saint Paul says, "if one member is honored, all rejoice together with it" (1 Cor 12:26).

Part of our collective work is to acknowledge that the Orthodox Church can get things wrong. The Orthodox Church is imperfect. The Orthodox Church has specifically failed to respect and care for women in accordance with its own teachings. Most of the reactions I received to my first book, *Maternal Body*, were very positive, but there was a theme among the few negative reactions: those readers were unwilling to see that the Orthodox Church is imperfect in its earthly expression. This reaction alarms me. I do not expect all readers to resonate with my thinking or agree with my proposals for how the Orthodox Church ought to align teachings and practices as regard mothers or women. But denying, or ignoring, the fallibility and imperfection of the church is something else altogether. When the faithful mistakenly perceive the earthly church as perfect and unchanging, they make it into a golden calf, and a blind eye is then turned to human weakness and sinfulness that includes not just matters relating to women, but other matters as well, such as sexual abuse and the misuse and abuse of authority.[5] The church that we actualize is necessarily imperfect because *we* are imperfect and still subject to sin as we journey through this life to the kingdom of heaven. From its divine origin, the church is perfect. We work toward that perfection, but do not yet fully experience it. To acknowledge that we are on this side of perfection allows us to move closer to it. Part of that work has to do with the roles and realities of women.

Some who argue against any change regarding women in the Orthodox Church today sound the alarm about "division," saying that, for example, reinstituting deaconesses will "divide" the Church. We ought not worry about potential division in the

---

5. See Deville, *Everything Hidden*, for the best and most constructive discussion to date on the abuse of authority in the church today.

Orthodox Church resulting from aligning its practices with its teachings. When this alignment happens, the Church will be a truer, better version of itself, this is an unquestionable good and division is not a concern.

Furthermore, there is already *a silent schism* at work in the Orthodox Church, as women and men who grew up in it leave.[6] Particularly young adults, but also Orthodox of all ages, see women excelling and appreciated in all aspects of contemporary society but treated as second-class citizens in the Orthodox Church. The Orthodox Church is the glaring and untenable exception in their minds. When they ask why the Orthodox Church limits and degrades women, they are often given poor, incorrect, or unsatisfying answers. I hear some version of this story all the time. Are these people leaving based the standards of the wider culture, rather than the standards of the Orthodox Church? Possibly so, but their convictions are in alignment with the standards of the Orthodox Church itself, because there is no theological, moral, dogmatic, or pastoral reason for the Orthodox Church's current treatment and status of women.

The reasoning in this book is based on the standards of the Orthodox Church itself, not the standards of contemporary society. There is no argument here for conformity with, or capitulation to, societal trends. The Orthodox Church is countercultural, after all; we believe that the divine entered human form, was born, taught, died, and rose again. Those who wish to dig their heels in and not change the Orthodox Church because of the massive change happening in the world are advocating a particular form of capitulation to societal trends: "Let's not change because the world around is changing so fast." Instead, the metric ought to be "What should we change and what should stay the same to best live out the fullness and truth of our faith?"

Meaningful change will require bravery and imagination. This book is one such effort. In it I envision the Orthodox Church I

---

6. A recent survey indicates that "only 12% of the regularly participating American Orthodox Church members are young adults (18–34)." Assembly of Bishops, "Orthodox Churches." This age group meanwhile constitutes 23% of the US population. U.S. Census Bureau, "American Community Survey."

would like, not just for my own future granddaughters, but for everyone's granddaughters, for *our* granddaughters, yours and mine (and our grandsons). Truly, it is the church I would like today for myself. Yet my lifetime of experience with the Orthodox Church informs my timescale. Even when courage and creativity are present, the Orthodox world is not known for swiftness. Sometimes this is a virtue. And transformative work rightfully takes time and care. Hence, I envision, hope, and pray these changes will be made within two generation's time.

# APPRECIATION

Recognition of my sources of inspiration, mentors, colleagues, and friends who have been formative in my thinking and methodology belongs here in the introduction (rather than only tucked away in the acknowledgments). First and foremost, I look to God. Jesus Christ's message of the dignity, value, and uniqueness of all human beings guides me. Christ's consistent care, attention, and respect toward women throughout his life gives me hope. I am informed by the lives of women in the early church: the pivotal presence of women in house churches, the creation of the order of deaconesses, and words such as Saint Basil's about men and woman: "The natures are alike of equal honor, the virtues are equal, the struggle equal, the judgment alike."[7]

I am inspired by the cloud of witnesses around me and especially women saints. Ever present with me when I wrote this book were two Saint Olgas. Olga of Kiev, in her formidable fortitude and visionary intelligence, creatively paved the way for Christianity to flourish in Slavic lands and she today stokes my own creativity and courage. Olga of Alaska, in her humble service to those around her, reminds me that my role—though expressed differently—is to serve the church in order to better the world.

I am guided by the piety and engagement of recent Orthodox theologians, such as Elisabeth Behr-Sigel and Saint Mother Maria Skobtsova, who lived out unique expressions of womanhood in the

7. Basil, "Origin of Humanity, Discourse 1," 18.

Church. I am also guided by scholars who have worked to clarify the history and possibility of women's ministry, including Valerie Karras and Kyriaki Karidoyanes Fitzgerald, as well as Phyllis Zagano, writing from the Catholic perspective. I am grateful for the perspectives garnered from my students—both at Western Washington University and Saint Sophia Ukrainian Orthodox Seminary—this book is stronger because of my time in the classroom.

I am supported and sustained by the wisdom and spiritual strength of my peers who are working to better the conditions of women in the Orthodox Church, including Patricia Fann Bouteneff, Rachel Contos, Susan Ashbrook Harvey, Dee Jaquet, Eleni Kasselouri-Hatzivasiliadi, Kyra Limberakis, Elena Narinskaya, Ashley Purpura, Elizabeth Prodromou, Marilyn Rouvelas, Caren Stayer, and Gayle Woloschak. This category includes those who serve the board of Saint Phoebe Center for the Deaconess with me—Kristina Baktis, Ann Marie Mecera, Gust Mecera, Teva Regule, Susan Smoley, Helen Theodoropoulos, and Sara Tsugranis—as well as the working group with whom I worked for a decade to revise the Churching prayers—Mary Ann DeTrana, Sasha Safchuk, Valerie Zahirsky, and, may their memories be eternal, Stefanie Yazge and Daria Petrykowski. I am also grateful for the loving women of my hometown parish, Saint Mary's Orthodox Church of Elkhorn/Bluefield, West Virginia.

I am inspired by women of other traditions because their experiences and work give me valuable perspectives on my own. One example is Rita Gross, the great Buddhist scholar-practitioner who patiently and methodically demonstrated the androcentric and oppressive practices and ideas about women in Buddhism and in the academy, and, in so doing, effected a path for real and lasting change, both confessional and academic, and also my teacher Karen Lang, who introduced me to Gross. Vanessa Ochs inspires with me her own work in ritual change in Judaism and woke me up when she said to me regarding my own, parallel work: "Write everything down because *you are making history.*" Personal friends belong in this category, too, including my spiritual sisters Holly Loth and Carolyn McCarthy and two dear Lutheran pastor friends: Jana Schofield and Sarah Hinlicky Wilson. I am also sincerely grateful for men in the Orthodox Church who see the need for women's situations to change and are also working, in one way or another, in this vineyard—you know who you are.

I am especially grateful for Orthodox friends who, like the words of Saint Ignatius, "labor together with one another, compete together, run together, suffer together, lie down together, and [are] raised up together as the household slaves, attendants, and servants of God,"[8] including Elizabeth Lincoln Bowman; Virginia Chryssikos; the entire Dunaway clan, but especially the matriarch and patriarch, Betsy and Fr. Marc; Laura Jansson; Jenni Malyon; Emily Schulte, Stefanie Siebeking; Elizabeth Scott Tervo; Pam Wright; and especially my own beloved and inspiring daughters, Annie, Eliza, and Beatrix.

Most influential of all was my own late mother, Menodora. She gave me her profound love and encouragement, the example of her own piety and compassion, and the example of working to fix what is broken even when your efforts are unappreciated or unpopular.

## STRUCTURE

This book is divided into six chapters, each of which addresses a major area in need of attention in the Orthodox Church concerning women: "Woman and Man," "Menstruation," "Churching," "Miscarriage," "Leadership," and "Ordination." The chapters are constructed in the same pattern: after introductory comments, I briefly illustrate the history of the theme in the Orthodox Church's past in one section and its present realities in another. The final section of each chapter speaks to the church of our granddaughters as I constructively share my hopes for the alignment of the Orthodox Church's practice with its teachings in two generation's time. Anecdotes from my own personal experience elucidate women's experiences for my reader (these anecdotes also reveal that my primary experience of the Orthodox Church is in the United States, even as my concern for the Orthodox Church is global). Footnotes

---

8. Ignatius of Antioch, "Letter to Polycarp," 6.

include citations and scholarly discussion that will be of interest to some readers.

"Woman and Man" covers various theological attempts to understand and describe what it means to be sex-differentiated as male and female, including my own model based on the Incarnation. It is the most theologically technical chapter. "Menstruation," "Churching," and "Miscarriage" deal with theologically indefensible prayers and practices relating to purity concerns around women's bodies and pose a model for leaving this dross behind. "Leadership" and "Ordination" focus on women's ministries, including their roles in governance and leadership and questions regarding women's ordination to the diaconate and the priesthood. Final thoughts about the future of women in the Orthodox Church appear in the conclusion.

## METHODS

My aim as a constructive theologian is to be faithful to the teachings of the Orthodox Church while acknowledging and engaging two realities. First, theology is an ongoing and creative process. Though we look to our theological tradition for guidance on any given topic, we can and should continue to develop theological ways of thinking addressing today's new questions (and timeless questions, too). Second, the Orthodox Church lives out its teachings imperfectly, especially as concerns the lives of women. Indeed, these imperfections, as I will elucidate, are often the result of a lack of faithfulness to Orthodox teachings.

My treatment of these matters is informed by my convictions about the process and goals of the interpretation of tradition. Often scholarship on women and the church seeks to reconcile disparate parts of a tradition. This mode prioritizes consistency, pursuing complete concordance of ideas to make everything match or fit or say the same thing. It includes the conviction that different, even contradictory, aspects of a tradition can be reconciled, and it places a premium on the effort to foster such reconciliation. This emphasis on consistency is inadequate, misguided, and requires hermeneutical gymnastics. Instead of perfect consistency, we ought to be seeking the truth.

This is not always easy. The tradition of the Orthodox Church is complex, rich, and multivalent. It includes scripture, theological treatises, homilies, canons, letters, iconography, liturgy, and hymnography. Some aspects of Orthodoxy are dogmatic, meaning universal in understanding and application, especially as related to the nature of God and humanity's relationship with God expressed by the seven ecumenical councils. Simultaneously, there are aspects to our tradition that simply contradict each other and therefore cannot be made to say the same thing without doing an injustice to the sources. We must be willing to discern which contradictory aspects are faithful to the teachings of the Orthodox Church—which are *true*—and which are not.

For example, the early church grappled with the question of what, if any, Levitical regulations should be continued. Some supported an understanding that the law was fulfilled by Jesus Christ and thus the Levitical regulations were moot for Christians. Others sought to preserve only the Levitical regulations having to do with women's bodies (see chapter 2). An approach that prioritizes consistency within tradition insists there is a logical cohesion to these different views. Case in point: Fr. Alexander Schmemann told his students that blood taboos for women were preserved because of the holiness women experience in their powers of co-creation with God. In this thinking, it made sense to keep only the Levitical purification practices having to do with women because of their reproductive prowess. In addition to the priority of consistency, in this case interpretive gymnastics are also required. There is no support within Orthodox Church thinking or ritual to suggest that women during their times of reproductive bleeding were perceived as especially holy.[9] The dissonance in these different messages about impurity and women's bodies indicates that something is awry. When considered in light of the fulfillment of the law by Jesus Christ, who cast categories of impurity into the realm of sin not

---

9. See chapter 4, "Postpartum," in my *Maternal Body* for a longer discussion of the history and interpretation of Levitical rules regarding women.

circumstance, female ritual impurity is clearly not truth-based and ought to be expunged from our thinking and practice.

Not only is consistency impossible within the Orthodox tradition when it comes to understandings of women, consistency has never been an Orthodox Christian priority. The richness and complexity of the Orthodox tradition cannot be neatly resolved. We know how to live with a certain amount of tension and ambiguity in this life and any insistence on perfect uniformity of the Orthodox Church's thoughts and practices reduces our faith to a caricature of itself. A more generous and creative mode of interpretation is needed, one that involves new, truth-seeking perspectives and approaches while being faithful to enduring Orthodox principles. Furthermore, as Christians we ought to be willing to call out parts of our tradition that are lacking or untrue. Doing so is not a compromise or failure of tradition, but a clarification and deepening of our convictions. It is an allegiance to tradition because it gets us closer to living out the truth.

Because truth-seeking interpretation does not primarily value consistency, it frees us from labored, apologetic, and polemical readings of tradition. The limitations and imperfections of tradition can be acknowledged. These include the limitations and imperfections of an Orthodox Church in which male interests and perspectives form nearly all of our textual tradition and other sources of theological information. Interpretive efforts within the Church have been executed largely by men, all accompanied with an underlying assumption that men are the rightful arbiters of tradition.

Truth-seeking interpretation involves an encounter with tradition that includes discernment and the guidance of the Holy Spirit. It acknowledges the ongoing, ever-unfolding process of our encounter with our Creator. It accepts that we cannot find wholecloth answers to our contemporary questions about women, men, or sex differentiation when we consult only patristic sources. Truth-seeking uses the God-given talents of imagination, intelligence, and creativity and allows for new but faithful readings of tradition by valuing new perspectives, including those of women. These perspectives include not only the work of women scholars but the reported *experiences* of women, which are often overlooked and undervalued. For the purposes of this book, truth-seeking interpretation allows the Orthodox Church to constructively consider the lives of its women.

## CHURCH OF OUR GRANDDAUGHTERS

I love the Orthodox Church. I also care for women and am committed to bettering their lives. These two starting places—my love for the church and my concern for women—create the central friction of this book, because the Orthodox Church fails to live up to its teachings and commitments when it comes to women and this failure damages women and the entire community. I write with hope, looking to a more fully realized future for women in the Orthodox Church and a better future for the whole church and its ministry in the world. By looking to the church of our "granddaughters," I convey this book's concern with women's roles and realities in the Orthodox Church, but this book is just as much for our grandsons as our granddaughters.

1

# Woman and Man

*I envision women understood and treated as fully human*
*persons who are appreciated for their own realities as women*
*in the church of our granddaughters.*

At an Orthodox institute this past summer a man asked me, "What does the Orthodox Church teach about the meaning of men and women?" I answered his question as well as I could, and he responded, "It sounds like the Church needs to do some more work." He felt that Orthodox thinking on sex and gender is incomplete and inadequate for our times. I assured him that I agree and that we are in good company: +Metropolitan Kallistos Ware (1934–2022) suggested many times that theological anthropology—the understanding of who we are as human beings, including considerations of sex differentiation and gender—ought to be the primary focus of Orthodox theology in the twenty-first century.

In this chapter, I consider past and present modes of such theological anthropology and I offer an alternative way of understanding sex differentiation in theological terms. This involves getting into complex issues, making this the most challenging, theologically technical chapter of the book. I've confined many examples and elaborations to the footnotes to minimize the jargon and maximize the clarity of the chapter. The questions themselves are straightforward, even if not easily answered. What is the theological significance of humanity's appearance in two sexes which are expressed in culturally influenced genders?[1] And what might this mean for women and men in the Orthodox Church today?

## WOMAN AND MAN: PAST

Several foundational but opaque passages from scripture address the significance of human sex differentiation into male and female. The first creation account presented in Genesis portrays humans as created male and female: "In the image of God he created them; male and female he created them" (Gen 1:27). The second chapter of Genesis offers a somewhat different version of the creation of humanity, with the woman being created from man's own body with the resulting comment from the man: "This at last is bone of my bones and flesh of my flesh; this one shall be called Woman, for out of Man this one was taken" (Gen 2:23).[2] In the New Testament, Saint Paul describes baptism as including an equalizing and liberating effect: "There is no longer male and female; for all of you are one in Christ Jesus" (Gal 3:28). The Orthodox Church has interpreted these passages (and others) in a variety of ways, yet it has never formulated dogma or formal doctrine concerning a theology of the sexes or a theology of gender.[3]

A note on nomenclature: throughout the book, I purposely differentiate the terms "the sexes" and "sex differentiation" from the term "gender." By the sexes or sex differentiation, I refer to the expression of humans as male and female represented by, but not limited to, biological and physical characteristics. By gender I

1. In parts of the world, questions about stability, fluidity, and mutability characterize contemporary discussions of sex differentiation and gender. I acknowledge these questions and perceive that the Orthodox Church, which does not reduce sex and gender to either biological or social epiphenomena, has much to offer, but my focus here is otherwise.

2. For a discussion of the translation issues around the two Genesis passages, see Bouteneff, *Beginnings*, 11.

3. For a longer description of Orthodox interpretations of these passages and general Orthodox understandings of gender, see Butcher, "Gender and Orthodox Theology," 25–46.

reference the socially and culturally understood roles of the sexes. My main concern is sex differentiation and its significance, knowing that what it means to be male and female is vital to Orthodox perspectives on women and that any Orthodox understanding of gender will flow from an understanding of sex differentiation.[4]

Theological concerns about sex differentiation are largely questions of our own time. The ancient church—to which we would naturally look for reflection on any topic—is more concerned with what it means to be a human person. This concern for the person is the natural foundation for reflection on the sexes. A person is created by God, unique, precious, infinitely important, and called to eternity. Yet, any description of the human person is incomplete and limited because "personhood cannot be exactly defined, . . . we cannot offer a systematic and exhaustive description. We do not fully understand what are the limits of our human nature, what are the possibilities as yet latent within it,"[5] in the words of Met. Kallistos.

A few patristic thinkers did wander beyond concerns of personhood into discussions of the sexes or gender. Some conjectured as to the reason for sex differentiation and its place, or lack of place, in God's plan for human beings. Others attributed certain qualities to men and women, reflective of the social structures of their own times and places. These reflections were not extensive, and none of them is accepted by the Orthodox Church as a universal truth (though they have influenced today's discussions of the sexes, as discussed below).

Even with the priority of emphasis on personhood, simultaneously, women and men are "equal" in the Incarnation.[6] Gregory of Nazianzus wrote, "Did He die for the Man? The Woman also is

4. To this end, I do not address "sex" in terms of physical, sexual acts or "sexuality" in terms of sexual inclinations. Though these things are no doubt related to sexual differentiation and gender and further reflection on them is certainly called for in an Orthodox context, my focus is sex differentiation.

5. Ware, "Foreword," 6.

6. I place "equal" in quotation marks to show its use is provisional; the word "equal" is difficult in an Orthodox context because it is now laden with contemporary human rights associations. I use "equal" to mean that both sexes are fully human, those for whom the Incarnation, death, and Resurrection of Jesus Christ are equally meaningful and applicable.

saved by His death. . . . They two, He says, shall be one Flesh; so let the one flesh have equal honor."[7] In this sample of patristic thinking, the "equal honor" and the mutual significance of Jesus Christ is for both sexes.

Sex differentiation is not a category that belongs to God, but instead belongs to humanity. This principle is established in the common patristic interpretation of Genesis 1:27, which views this passage in an inclusive sense, meaning God created *both* male *and* female in God's image.[8] We are to understand God not through human experience but instead seek to understand humans through what we know about God, knowing that humans are created for and through relationship with God. Any view or portrayal of God as sex differentiated is problematic because it overlays expressly human qualities onto God, who is beyond human qualities. This might seem to get sticky in the Incarnation, because Jesus Christ incarnates as a male human born of a woman, but it is his humanity that is sexed, not his divinity.[9]

The interpretation of Genesis tells us that sex differentiation necessarily characterizes humanity; we are, in fact, sexed from our creation as male and female. But what is the meaning or significance of being male and female? Does each sex have its own *essential* way of being human; its own traits or characteristics that can be named and defined? By "essential" or "essentialist" I mean qualities that are inherent, inborn, determinative, and purposefully of the essence of our creation and our deification.[10] What does sex differentiation, so

7. Gregory of Nazianzus, "Discourse 37."

8. See Karras, "Patristic Views," 113–19.

9. As we consider sex differentiation and God, it is important to point out that the Orthodox Church has often used gendered pronouns to refer to God. There is no personal, non-gendered pronoun in English and yet God is three persons in trinity, so a personal pronoun is necessary. Most commonly masculine words or pronouns are used in English, but across church tradition, there are also examples of feminine words and pronouns used to refer to God. See Harvey, "Feminine Imagery," 111–39.

10. Many theologians use the term "ontological" instead of "essential" in discussions of sex differentiation and gender. I prefer "essential" or "essentialist" for its simplicity and clarity and because I'm not convinced "ontological" has one stable definition in the context of Orthodox theology. All of the

central to our human experience, mean? Why does it matter? This brings us to the conundrum: humans are sex differentiated, God is not, and yet we are to somehow discern the meaning of human sex differentiation in light of God. How might we go about this?

## WOMAN AND MAN: TODAY

A few qualities are necessary for successful, twenty-first-century considerations of sex differentiation. One is an appreciation for the first principles of the Orthodox understanding of the sexes outlined above. Another is the willingness to venture beyond the patristic thinkers' musings, knowing that we cannot ask them to say more than they have. Their thinking on the sexes is incomplete given the lack of priority of these topics in their own time and because of the different context and language used around sex differentiation and gender today. Reflection on these matters requires a constructive approach that is both faithful to tradition and creative.

Today, there are two general models in thinking about sex differentiation within Orthodox Christianity. I term them as the "edenic" and the "eschatological." These models tend toward the extreme, and I will present an alternative after first elucidating each.

The edenic derives its ideal of sex differentiation from the depictions and interpretations of the garden of Eden in Genesis before the Fall. It views man and woman as complementary and sex differentiation as part of God's original plan. In this thinking, the bifurcation of humans into two sexes is a God-given opportunity for human beings to participate in reciprocal partnership, in love, which is linked with marriage. Some passages in Genesis are typically referenced, such as: "Therefore a man leaves his father and his mother and clings to his wife, and they become one flesh" (Gen 2:24). Some proponents of the edenic model understand that sex differentiation may persist, in some form, in the next life.

Often edenic thinking involves an "essentialist" view of the sexes, the idea that male and female each have identifiable,

---

passages I quote in this chapter that use "ontological" do so in a way that I interpret as compatible with my use of "essential."

different, and usually complementary characteristics or "charisms" that are innate to and definitive of each sex.[11] Much current Orthodox Christian edenic thinking can be traced back to twentieth-century Orthodox theologian Fr. Thomas Hopko, who articulated and defended essentialism.[12] Some expressions of Orthodox essentialism include a "different but equal" quality, but articulations of Orthodox essentialism often involve the subordination of women to men based on a hierarchal understanding of humanity,[13] and this thinking is used to justify limited roles and opportunities for women (such as excluding women from leadership roles and ordained orders,[14] see chapters 5 and 6) and continued ritual disparagement of women (such excommunication during menstruation and derogatory language in the Churching and Miscarriage prayers, see chapters 2–4).

11. Karras explains complementarity and its drawbacks and urges us to question views of extreme immanence as well as views of extreme transcendence when thinking about these things, similar to the way I question the edenic and eschatological extremes. Karras, "Eschatology," 246.

12. See Hopko, "God and Gender," 141–83.

13. For an Orthodox argument for essentialist/ontological-based subordination of women, see Farley, *Feminism and Tradition*, and read the response of Ladouceur, review of *Feminism and Tradition*. A parallel development of essentialist and hierarchical understandings of the sexes took place in other Christian communities in the second half of the twentieth century. Much would be learned from a study of the ways such thinking in the Orthodox Church was influenced by these developments. For a discussion of this history in evangelical Christianity, see Shaw, "Gracious Submission."

14. For example, the late Orthodox counselor and priest Fr. George Morelli wrote, "God could and did choose to start the human race with a male, Adam, giving him ontological priority; . . . in the most basic sense, man in relation to woman is a given, a particular way of imaging God as Father and Son. Woman is the accompanying receiver, exercising her image of God with freedom, dignity, and honor. This leads to our understanding, for example, of the ordained priesthood of the church being properly exercised by males as loving heads." Morelli, "Biopsychology of Sexuality," 110. The thinking of Morelli and others that only men can be priests because of their ontological headship is sometimes extended into the syllogism that only men can represent Christ in the liturgy, meaning Christ was a man, therefore only men can be icons of Christ and therefore only men can be priests. See chapter 6 for a full discussion of women and ordination.

There are several problems with the edenic model of sex differentiation. Its commitment to certain masculine traits as definitive of men and certain feminine traits as of women is reductive, narrowing, and limits the sexes at the expense of the full expression of each human person.[15] For example, when we speak of men as "active" and women as "passive" (even when activity and passivity are both portrayed positively), we diminish their personhood by pigeonholing them into preconceived categories. Thus, we negate the chance for them to perceive and grow in their own, personal gifts, and we limit their participation in society and the church. Furthermore, proponents of the edenic rarely acknowledge that their proposed attributes for male and female are historically and socially conditioned. These thinkers are deeply influenced by the gendered norms and ideals of their own time and place.

In its enthusiasm for essentialist qualities of the sexes, sometimes the edenic model departs from the principle that sex differentiation cannot be projected back onto the Godhead.[16] When essentialist thinking promotes certain innate traits of men in particular, shifting the emphasis from Christ's humanity to his maleness, the unfortunate implication is that the significance of the Incarnation might be only for men.[17]

The other trend in Orthodox thinking about sex differentiation is "eschatological," meaning chiefly concerned with the eschaton, the final things. In this thinking, sex differentiation is primarily understood as overcome in the next life.[18] The idea is that in the

15. Evdokimov's *Women and Salvation* is an example of a well-intentioned expression of essentialism, in which he set up some of these complementary dichotomies in his efforts to create a more productive conversation around women and sexuality.

16. Such as in the work of Hopko: "There is a direct, analogical, symbolic and epiphanic relationship between Adam [man] and the Son of God and between Eve [woman] and the Spirit of God." Hopko, "On the Male Character," 106.

17. Jesus Christ became incarnate as a male human being, but the salvific emphasis within Orthodox thinking is not on his maleness, but on his *humanity*. As Gregory of Nazianzus observed, "For that which He has not assumed He has not healed; but that which is united to His Godhead is also saved." Gregory of Nazaianzus, "Critique of Apollinarius and Apollinarianism."

18. An unusual example of the eschatological model is Fr. John Behr,

"spiritual bodies" (1 Cor 15:44) we will experience in the general resurrection, sex differentiation will no longer be present. Sex differentiation is something ephemeral, present only in this life and to be transcended, overcome, and perhaps elided entirely in the next.

Even with the focus on the end, eschatological views are nearly always informed by views of the beginning, the original creation of humans. These views are nearly the opposite to the edenic model. Rather than seeing sex differentiation as definitive of creation and definitive of what it means to be human, the eschatological view is that sex differentiation is absent from, or secondary to, God's plan for humanity and therefore has no significance.[19]

This thinking is often linked with Saint Gregory of Nyssa's ideas about a "double creation," in which sex differentiation is established out of God's foreknowledge or anticipation of the Fall.[20] In "double-creation," sex differentiation exists as a secondary trait

---

whose views on the sexes are highly eschatological in the sense that "becoming human" is only possible through death, though he gives some space for the significance of sex differentiation in this life. I am, ultimately, not comfortable with this model's eschatological view of what it means to be human; although becoming human may be understood as a process, I am not convinced that death is necessary to become human in an essential/ontological sense. Behr, "From Adam to Christ," 19–32.

19. Bishop Maxim Vasiljević asks, "Does gender have a future?" in one of the chapter titles in *Theology as Surprise*, and the answer for him appears to be "no," for eschatological reasons. Vasiljević, *Theology as Surprise*.

20. Gregory's thoughts on double creation were propositional and tentative, but the eschatological proponents often cite, interpret, or develop them as doctrinal. Even though his thinking is often invoked as support of the eschatological model because of his views of sex differentiation vis-à-vis the Fall, he also understood sex differentiation in some sense as deliberate and meaningful for human life—Fall or no Fall. This is expressed in his suggestion that the function of the sexes is to position humans in between the animals (which are sexed) and the divine (which is not sexed), as a microcosm of all creation. This draws upon the wider patristic view that humanity, bearing the image of God, is a microcosm of the spiritual, animal, and material. In this understanding, sex differentiation shared between humans and many animals works to integrate all of creation within and through human beings. This is a suggestive and promising line to follow in considerations of our relationship with the rest of the animal world and our understanding of our planet. See Bouteneff's discussion of Gregory's views in *Beginnings* and see Gregory's *On the Making of Man*.

to allow humans to "be fruitful and multiply" after the Fall (with an understanding that the mechanism of multiplication/procreation—if present at all—would have been more spiritual and less bodily in the event that humans did not fall). In this view, sometimes sex differentiation is understood to be present but meaningless in the garden and then activated in the Fall. Other times it is understood as absent from the garden, but manifest at the time of the Fall—these are Gregory of Nyssa's "garments of skin."[21] Either way, sex differentiation is a result of the Fall, and the upshot of eschatological thinking is the *insignificance* of sex differentiation.

In its favor, the eschatological model perceives sex differentiation as only concerning humans; it is not overlaid back onto our understanding of God. Yet, with its eagerness to perceive sex differentiation as insignificant comes a disproportionate interested in sexuality and creation in this model. It is not a stretch to connect this focus to the fact that many of the patristic thinkers who are cited to support an eschatological model today were unmarried, male, celibate, sometimes monastic, and largely of the opinion that the life of consecrated virginity or monasticism was superior to the life of raising a family. Negative associations with, or, at best, ignorance of, procreation, family, and women would come naturally in this context. In the words of Elisabeth Behr-Sigel, "femininity was a synonym for weakness . . . and for the Christian elite, to which [Gregory of Nyssa] belonged, an elite powerfully influenced by the monastic movement, virginity preserved for the Lord was objectively superior to the state of married men and women."[22] In other sources from Orthodox tradition, including the marriage rite itself, procreation is often portrayed favorably,

21. The dependence on Gregory of Nyssa's double creation is concerning. He offered this idea as experimental and tentative and yet it is taken as foregone teaching in this model, even though the theory of double-creation is not dogmatic and potentially compromises human freedom, with connotations of predestination in its scheme of God's foreknowledge of the Fall.

22. Behr-Sigel, *Ministry of Women*, 87. It's interesting to remember that Gregory of Nyssa was himself a married man.

but it is never the central goal of human existence (or even marriage), which is, instead, deification.[23]

I am unsatisfied with both edenic and eschatological models of sex differentiation for many reasons. Both views are often linked with contemporary stances regarding cultural issues, suggesting that confirmation bias may be at work. Edenic proponents may present the essentialism of sex differentiation as support for male-dominated families and society as well as heterosexual relationships and marriage. Some edenic thinkers use this model to justify limited roles of women in the Orthodox Church, including the male-only priesthood. On the other hand, proponents of the eschatological may point to the ephemerality of sex differentiation as support for placing no value on sex differentiation today, which potentially leaves the door open for an acceptance of homosexual relationships and gender-less or gender-fluid norms. The emphasis on the insignificance of sex differentiation also lends itself to "gnostic" tendencies of our age: increasing wariness and denigration of the body at the expense of the full person with its intimate body and soul connection. Note that I am not expressing sanction or censure on the conclusions of either model. My concern is that their conclusions may be dictating their models, not the other way around.

The certainty claimed by both is uncomfortable. The edenic claims to clearly understand the original, God-created model of sex differentiation before the Fall. The eschatological claims certainty around both the future and the past, asserting that sex differentiation is meaningless in the next life and was only a bug, not a feature, of the original creation. Yet, both beginnings and ends are ultimately unknowable to us. Both models are extremely speculative. Both are also flawed in their shared and unstated assumption that humans are static, either in the garden or in the life to come. Orthodox thinking about personhood includes the possibility for growth and change.

A final reason for dissatisfaction with these models is that they are both created exclusively *by men*. The Orthodox Church cannot

23. It is the unitive goods of marriage, the possibility of the married couple growing in deification together, that is the primary purpose of marriage. See Guroian, "Ethic of Marriage and Family."

effectively rise to Metropolitan Kallistos's challenge to approach theological anthropology this century using only the thoughts and perceptions of men (almost all of them celibate and/or clerical). Perhaps not accidentally, both perspectives also distinctly *benefit* men.[24] The edenic perspective allows for men in the Orthodox Church to continue to subordinate women at worst, or narrowly circumscribe women in quasi-theological categories of essentialism at best. The eschatological model benefits men because if sex differentiation doesn't ultimately matter, then women's concerns, realities, and experiences can continue to be dismissed, diminished, or ignored in the Orthodox Church.

For Orthodox theological anthropology to be better articulated, women must be a part of the conversation. Contemporary women theologians and scholars must also be included, as well as women who have gone before us. I look forward to the decades to come as more women work in this field. In the meantime, I offer my own provisional thoughts.

## WOMAN: THE CHURCH OF OUR GRANDDAUGHTERS

I propose that rather than focusing on the beginning (Eden) or the end (eschaton), the "middle" we are living in now ought to shape our understanding of sex differentiation. Our reality is an "incarnational reality," meaning we are defined not exclusively by our beginnings or ends, but by our existence in light of the Incarnation. We live in the "middle"—in between Eden and eschaton—in the era of Incarnation; in incarnational time that is revealed in the person of Christ but already present in the first humans and witnessed by the holy men and women of Israel. This incarnational reality has consequences for the whole human person, sexual differentiation included.

24. Even as these views were originally formulated by men and benefit men, they are certainly held in contemporary times by some women. For an example of the edenic, see Kyriaki Fitzgerald's remarks quoted in Butcher's "Gender and Orthodox Theology," 37. Consider also Elisabeth Behr-Sigel's views on sexual differentiation and gender and how these views changed over the course of her lifetime; see Wilson, *Woman, Women, and the Priesthood*.

When we look at our incarnational reality, an "incarnational model" of sex differentiation and gender becomes possible.[25] In an incarnational model, sex differentiation is understood as having to do with humans—not the traits of God—and humans as expressly understood through the Incarnation. The universally salvific principle of the Incarnation does not bind and reduce humans to narrow categories defined by their sex. Furthermore, Jesus Christ blessed our incarnational reality of human sexual differentiation by himself being sexed.

The incarnational model re-orients discussions of sex differentiation in terms of the Incarnation, which has been omitted from both the edenic and the eschatological. This is the most significant lacuna in both models—their focus on beginnings or ends to the exclusion of the cosmos-changing events of the middle, the Incarnation.[26] In a incarnational model, questions of whether sex differentiation persists in the next life, or is part of the original, ideal creation, or is a massive plan B hedging against the Fall (all of which are unknowable) are secondary to our experience of being human in light of the Incarnation, which is, in many ways, knowable.

Viewing sex differentiation in light of the Incarnation appreciates each person as unique, precious, irreplaceable, called to eternity, and newly sanctified by all the events of the Incarnation: the birth, teaching, death, crucifixion, and Resurrection of Christ. It also accepts that we cannot offer a complete description of a human person, much less of man or woman. There is room for mystery and possibility. Through the Incarnation, deification—to become Christ-like and commune with God in the kingdom—is open to every human. Thus, in the incarnational model, everyone

25. To clarify, the "Incarnation" refers to Jesus Christ's presence on earth as fully human and fully God; our "incarnational reality" refers to our lives as humans as understood through Jesus Christ's Incarnation; and the "incarnational model" refers to a way of understanding ourselves, including sex differentiation, in light of the Incarnation.

26. Karras brings a lot of clarity and creates a useful framework in her list of the stages of the creation of humans, but even within these, she does not discuss the significance of the Incarnation for sex differentiation. See "Patristic Views."

is appreciated for their person and their gifts, all within the body of Christ. In the words of Saint Paul,

> For as in one body we have many members, and not all the members have the same function, so we, who are many, are one body in Christ, and individually we are members of one another. We have gifts that differ accordingly to the grace given to us: prophecy, in proportion to faith; ministry, in ministering; the teacher, in teaching; the exhorter, in exhortation; the giver, in generosity; the leaders in diligence; the compassionate, in cheerfulness. (Rom 12:6–8)

While an incarnational model rejects an essentialist quality to sex differentiation, it deeply values our experience of ourselves as humans differentiated into two sexes. The emphasis on the "middle"—our incarnational reality—acknowledges that humans are sex differentiated and that this is meaningful in light of the Incarnation: meaningful in our lived experience and meaningful to our deification. Sex differentiation is real but cannot be, and does not need to be, defined or demarcated. Just as we cannot fully define the person because of magnitude and mystery, so too we cannot define a systematic, exhaustive, or even helpful description of male or female qualities. The incarnational model also avoids the trappings of biological reductionism that defines and limits sex differentiation and human experience to solely physical attributes. Instead, consideration of the full human being is possible—the body, the mind, the spirit.

I freely acknowledge that my thinking on an incarnational model for understanding sex differentiation might well be bound up with my own incarnational reality as a woman. And perhaps especially as a mother. Our tradition often cites the troika of crucifixion, death, and Resurrection as foundational for our understanding of reality. I see the importance of adding in Jesus Christ's *birth and life* and therefore more fully appreciating the implications of the Incarnation for our own lives. I also acknowledge that I am not immune to confirmation bias; my ideas about the sexes are included in a book about improving the future for women in the Orthodox Church, after all. Yet, in my thinking about the significance of sex differentiation, I have sought a pragmatic and constructive view that honors the principles of theological anthropology, that is informed by the Incarnation, and that includes the actual experience of being a woman or a man. Even though we understand ourselves to be equal in the Incarnation, our lives tell us we are not equivalent.

The incarnational model allows us to work with what we know, our own experience of being human—body, mind, and soul—acknowledging that sex differentiation is directly relevant to our lives. It frees us to explore our own experience of sex differentiation, with all the tools available to us, including new scientific knowledge of the sexes and ideas and theories around the construction of gender. It neither limits us to essentialist qualities of each sex nor to cultural constructions of gender roles but instead allows us to explore our own realities and experiences. It means we can ask what aspects of Orthodoxy today are determined by cultural and social ideas of the sexes in comparison to an incarnational understanding of these things. With this model, we can accept both Saint Paul's understanding in Romans of gifts belonging to each human person and also hear his words in Galatians as descriptive of the equalizing, liberating effect of baptism on everyone, not necessarily the elision of the sexes: "As many of you were baptized into Christ have clothed yourself in Christ. There is no longer Jew or Greek, there is no longer slave or free, there is no longer male or female; for all of you are one in Christ Jesus" (Gal 3:27–28).

"All one in Christ Jesus" is the root of the incarnational model. The Christ-immersed first principle of our mysterious and beautiful humanity ought to be the foundation of any investigation of sex differentiation. With this foundation, an exploration of the experience of being woman and man on this side of the Incarnation is possible. Sex differentiation is not essentialist, but it is *existentially significant*.[27] Sex differentiation is important because it has so much to do with our experiences of this life, and thus our path to deification.

27. This is a bit of a paraphrase of Thermos, who wrote, "Gender is not an ontological entity, but it serves an ontological mission." Thermos, "Sexual Orientation and Gender," 88. Thermos uses the word "gender," rather than sex and uses the term "ontological," which I do not. I interpret his thinking as in line with my own, but paraphrase here rather than quote him due to differences in terminology and wishing to avoid misrepresenting his thinking.

The incarnational realities of women have been diminished or ignored by the Orthodox Church, and the Orthodox Church suffers as a result. Current roles and experiences of women in the Orthodox Church are not based on its core understanding of humanity, but instead are reflections of larger cultural patterns and expressions of gender—many of which are, in fact, *antithetical* to Orthodox theological anthropology. We have not yet experienced an Orthodox Church in which "we are all one in Christ Jesus" because we have not experienced the full integration of women into the life of the Orthodox Church. It is my hope that the Orthodox Church will fully incorporate women's incarnational realities into the body of Christ. It is my hope that our granddaughters will know that their lives are not strictly determined by their sex, and simultaneously appreciate, and be appreciated for, their incarnational realities as women in the Orthodox Church.

# 2

# Menstruation

*I envision all women and girls welcomed at the chalice in the*
*church of our granddaughters, with no conditions on their*
*reception of the Eucharist based on the biological cycles of*
*their female bodies.*

It took the perspective of an adult for me to realize that my home-town parish was somewhat unusual. It was one of the earliest Slavic parishes to move to an all-English liturgy. Its yearly picnic included gambling and whiskey. And there was no prohibition on the women and girls coming to church during menstruation. I was in college before an Orthodox woman my age casually mentioned this phenomenon, which was news to me! I was shocked.

Since then, I've come to understand that in many parishes and areas of the Orthodox world, women and girls are excommunicated during menstruation. In some of these contexts, they are further-more instructed not to venerate icons, light candles or lamps, kiss the cross, bake prosphora, or engage in other acts of worship. Some menstruating women and girls are prohibited from coming to church at all.

My use of the term "excommunication" may seem exaggerated or melodramatic, but it is merely descriptive. It is a word of Latin extraction, with *ex* meaning "out of" and *communication* meaning "communication" or "communion," the entire term coming together to be "out of communion" or "excluded from communion." In the Orthodox context, excommunication is typically understood as an aspect of church discipline or order. Someone might be excommunicated for a grievous sin that temporarily estranges the person from the church community, with an eye to their return to the chalice after time and penance. Notably, they are not banned from the church community entirely but from reception of the Eucharist, which is very serious and painful indeed (total expulsion from the church community has a different term: *anathema*). Menstruating females, then, are properly described as "excommunicated"; this is the precise term for their status during their monthly period. But they are excommunicated for functions of their bodies, not for grievous sin.

This excommunication is the quintessential example of an Orthodox Christian practice that is out of step with the core teachings on women, the human body, and the Incarnation.

## MENSTRUATION: PAST

Part of the very early Christian journey was the interpretation of Jewish scripture and practice through the revelation of Jesus Christ and his teachings, including menstruation-related and other purity practices described in Leviticus (see, for example, Lev 15:19–24).[1] In the ancient Israelite context, simply put, "uncleanliness" or "impurity" referred to a state in which divine equilibrium was out of kilter but could be made right again through ritual action.[2]

1. "When a woman has a discharge of blood that is her regular discharge from her body, she shall be in her impurity for seven days, and whoever touches her shall be unclean until the evening. Everything upon which she lies during her impurity shall be unclean; everything also upon which she sits shall be unclean. Whoever touches her bed shall wash his clothes, and bathe in water, and be unclean until the evening. Whoever touches anything upon which she sits shall wash his clothes, and bathe in water, and be unclean until the evening; whether it is the bed or anything upon which she sits, when he touches it he shall be unclean until the evening. If any man lies with her, and her impurity falls on him, he shall be unclean seven days; and every bed on which he lies shall be unclean" (Lev 15:19–24).

2. For a discussion of how women and their bodies were understood under Jewish law and practice, see Biale, *Women and Jewish Law*.

But this was not the Christian understanding of impurity held by Jesus Christ, who fulfilled the law (Matt 5:17–20) and recast "impurity" as sinful language or actions.[3] Jesus Christ taught that it is not circumstance or bodily functions that defile, but actions and thoughts (Mark 7:15). Early church sources supported the view that menstruation does not bar women from the Eucharist or from church. The Didascalia Apostolorum, the third-century proto-canon law document, instructs: "For this cause therefore do you approach without restraint to those who are at rest, and hold them not unclean. In like manner also you shall not separate those [women] who are in the wonted [natural] courses; for she also who had the flow of blood was not chidden [chided] when she touched the skirt of our Savior's cloak but was even vouchsafed the forgiveness of all her sins."[4] Saint John Chrysostom proclaimed in the fourth century: "All things are pure. God made nothing unclean, for nothing is unclean, except in sin only. For that reaches to the soul and defiles it."[5]

Yet, despite Jesus Christ's examples and teachings, despite these clear convictions within the early church that Levitical purity law was fulfilled in the Christian context, and despite the Christian understanding of impurity as something brought on by sin, not circumstance, there were still some in the early church who wished to distinguish women's bodies as the *one exception* to the inapplicability of Levitical law.[6] Since then, the theologi-

---

3. Sometimes the traditional understanding of Mary's "excommunication" from the temple is referenced in defense of the menstruation excommunication. This detail of Mary's life comes not from the Gospels but from the third-century Protoevangelium of James. In it, Mary lives in the temple from age three, but must leave in her early adolescence due to the commencement of her menstrual cycle. Mary was an Israelite, she was a Jewish woman, and Levitical law applied to her. Nothing can be extended or concluded from this to justify the Orthodox Church's menstruation excommunications. See Protoevangelium of James 6.

4. Didascalia Apostolorum 22.

5. Chrysostom, "Homily 3 on Titus," ch. 1, v. 16.

6. There is inclusion in some prayer books of a prayer for the impurity associated with "nocturnal emissions of men." This is also troubling and indicates a discomfort with human sexuality in general. However, this prayer

cally spurious connection between impurity and women's bodies has reappeared at different times throughout church history. It is mentioned in theological texts, makes its way into church canons, and influences church practices.[7] Dionysius of Alexandria, for example, wrote a letter to a brother bishop in the middle of the third century approving of banning menstruating females from the Eucharist as well as from approaching the table from which the Eucharist is served.[8] This legacy eventually led to women and girls in the twenty-first century being told to abstain from the Eucharist during their periods.

Why, especially given the clear recasting of purity into the realm of free will by Jesus Christ and his fulfillment of Levitical law, is there such inconsistency in church teaching and practice? Orthodox scholar Sister Vassa Larin observes that teachings and practices never materialize in a vacuum, but instead appear "within the socio-cultural, historical reality of the ancient world."[9] She points out that sources aligned with Jesus Christ's teachings regarding purity, like Didascalia Apostolorum (mentioned above), tend to come from such places in the ancient world as Syria, where Christians were in conflict with the local Jewish population. In this setting, Christians tended to define themselves and their practices in strict accordance with Jesus's teaching on purity in order to emphasize the contrast with traditional Jewish practice. On the other hand, sources that supported the putative connection between women's bodies and impurity come from other places such as Egypt— such as Dionysius and his letter—where the Jewish and Christian

---

differs in many ways from that of the menstruation excommunication: one, it is rarely practiced today and often unknown; two, its practice in the past appears to have been limited; three, men are given the ability to discern whether such emission bans them from the chalice or not; and four, there is no public setting apart of men on a regular, visible basis.

7. See the discussion of where within a church it was permissible for menstruating women to stand in Taft, "Women at Church," 53.

8. Dionysius of Alexandria, *Letters*, 102–3.

9. Larin, "What Is 'Ritual Im/purity,'" 284–85.

populations peacefully coexisted at the time and thus the Christians tended to be influenced by Jewish purity categories.[10]

Whatever sympathy or understanding we might muster for the historical circumstances that linked concepts of impurity, defilement, and uncleanness together with menstruation, this link is simply invalid in the Christian context. Ideally, Christians would be true to the inner logic of their teachings on impurity/purity while living in respect and peace with the Jewish community. This is especially apparent when considered in light of Orthodox teachings regarding the human body and the Incarnation, which, unlike canons, transcend time and space. We take our bodily existence very seriously because our bodies are God-given and especially because our God himself deliberately took on a body; as second-century Saint Irenaeus expressed when describing Jesus and his Incarnation: "the only true and steadfast Teacher, the Word of God, our Lord Jesus Christ, who did, through His transcendent love, become what we are, that He might bring us to be even what He is Himself."[11] Jesus Christ became what we are so that we might become what he is.

The idea that humans are destined to become "what he is," to become like God—to experience "deification"—is central to the Orthodox Christian understanding of human life. The mind and spirit are intimately involved, but the workshop of deification is the body. God became human, became embodied, in order to experience a new intimacy with us, so that we might experience a new intimacy with him—within and through our bodies.

Orthodox Christian teachings and practices regarding menstruation have everything to do with how we truly perceive the Incarnation. Menstruation, the monthly evacuation of the uterine lining, does not temporarily compromise a woman's baptism. It is simply what happens to the fertile female body every month or so

10. Larin, "What Is 'Ritual Im/purity,'" 282. Others have suggested that these canons were initiated because of the historically poor quality of menstrual materials in the ancient world. See Liveris's discussion of FitzGerald's thinking on this topic in Liveris, *Ancient Taboos and Gender*, 146. I think this is not likely to be the dominant contributing factor, because, if it were, we would have more examples from the ancient world. If these canons are reflective of this problem of materials, then they are obsolete today.

11. Irenaeus, *Against Heresies*, V.

in the absence of a pregnancy. Excommunication on grounds of menstruation dismisses the centrality, the sacredness of the body. This dismissal of the female body is a denigration of the way we understand our bodies in light of the Incarnation. The church's theologians have long and robustly defended its Christology in councils, theological texts, and formulations. It is time to defend our Christology in *practice* when it comes to the treatment of the female body.

The Orthodox Church's incarnational and eucharistic theology transcends any canons or comments regarding women's bodies and their menstrual cycles. The human body is validated as worthy and sanctified by the Incarnation. Impurity is understood as sin and is cast into the sphere of choice, not circumstance. These things are just as true of women's bodies as they are of men's bodies—our understanding of the Incarnation depends upon it.

The importance of the Eucharist within Orthodox Christian life cannot be underestimated. Paul Evdokimov tells us that "there is no possible scale of comparison: . . . every sacrament depends on the power of the Eucharist, which is that of the Church itself."[12] It is sobering to consider the number of times women and girls have been disenfranchised of the body and blood of Christ over the centuries because of the Orthodox Church's failure to minister to half of its people.

When we consider the foundational truths about the significance our bodies and the Incarnation, we see clearly that the practice of banning girls and women from the Eucharist is both unChristian and terribly damaging. Orthodox scholar Leonie B. Liveris observes, "The enforcement [of these practices] is instilled in the psyche of women, already living and experiencing veracious insidious forms of patriarchy in their culture and traditions. The absence of a mother or teenage daughter from communion [or church entirely] at the end of Holy Week is quietly observed not only by immediate family but may be noted by friends and relatives at church."[13] This is both unnecessary and can produce embarrass-

12. Evdokimov, *Orthodoxy*, 272.

13. Liveris, *Ancient Taboos and Gender*, 82, 147.

ment or even shame about their bodies. The excommunication for menstruation portrays women's and girls' bodies as unworthy of the Eucharist for a significant portion of their lives. And because our personhood is bound up in our bodies, the clear message of this excommunication is that those of us with female bodies are less worthy than men of the Lord's body and blood.

I deliberately use the awkward construction "women and girls" throughout this chapter because I wish to draw attention to the fact that it is not just full-grown adult women being excommunicated from the chalice during their periods, but *children* are also being treated this way. The Orthodox Church has truly offended the "little ones" in perpetuating these practices (Luke 17:2). Jesus Christ admonished his disciples to not prohibit the children from coming to him (Matt 19:13–15), and the Eucharist is the ultimate "coming unto him." That the Orthodox Church would inflict this psychological and spiritual damage on girls is indefensible.

Another toll of the menstruation excommunication is the sometimes subtle and sometimes overt effect it has had over the centuries on perceptions of women as unworthy to minister; putative impurity from menstruation has been a reason cited for barring women from the minor or major orders. I will further explore this connection further in chapters 5 and 6.

## MENSTRUATION: TODAY

Menstruation excommunication practices related to the Eucharist in the United States today are highly variable from jurisdiction to jurisdiction, from parish to parish, even person to person. In some cases, the perpetration of these practices is coming from within a family and not from the clergy, yet still, the Orthodox Church and the clergy condone these practices by not pastorally counseling otherwise. In other cases, menstruation excommunication comes directly from the pulpit. I also know of parishes that have implicitly or explicitly abandoned menstruation excommunication practices; as mentioned in the beginning of the chapter, this was true at my hometown parish.

Notably, some figures who are staunchly opposed to the re-institution and expansion of women's ministerial roles in the Orthodox Church advocate at the same time for women's access to the Eucharist.[14] Yet, there are contemporary figures who do wish to perpetuate the menstruation excommunication. For example, Alice C. Linsley, an Orthodox anthropologist, takes a comparative religions/anthropological perspective, arguing that most traditions across time and space have upheld menstruation prohibitions due to the preservation of categorical binary distinctions; simply, women's blood cannot be in the same place as God. Specific to Christianity, menstruation and postpartum women thus cannot draw near to near God in the form of the Eucharist.[15] Her argument is not based on Christian sources and completely ignores the radical change the meaning of purity and impurity ushered in by Christ and his fulfillment of the law. Christianity is not equivalent to other traditions, no matter how widespread; the entirety of Christian truth is bound up in the reconciliation of a binary—God and humanity—through the Incarnation.[16]

The Russian Orthodox Church has recently taken dramatic moves to condone and perpetuate the excommunication from the chalice in a 2015 statement, "On the Participation of the Faithful in the Eucharist approved by the Russian Synod": "The canons prohibit receiving communion in the state of female impurity (canon 2 of Saint Dionysius of Alexandria, canon 7 of Timothy of Alexandria). An exception may be made in case of a danger of death, and whenever the issue of blood continues for a long time due to chronic or acute illness."[17] The two sources referenced are from third- and fourth-century Alexandria, both written in a context very different than contemporary Russia. The Russian Orthodox Church today is not in the position of Dionysius, influenced by a Jewish

14. See, for example, Farley, "Menstruation and Communion of Women."

15. Linsley, "Stepping into the Stream," 31–34.

16. Linsley's thinking also supports banning females from the altar on the putative association between menstruation and incompatibility with the body and blood of Christ—an argument that does not measure up to the Orthodox Church's incarnational theology.

17. Russian Orthodox Church, "On Participation of the Faithful."

community. This may be one of many examples of the post-Soviet Russian Church reflexively holding tight to preexisting traditions and rituals, regardless of their theological legitimacy.[18]

In contrast, other Orthodox churches are taking the opposite approach. In 1997, the Synod of Antioch proclaimed:

> The Holy Synod discussed matters which touch the lives of women and decided that women and men should be treated equally concerning their participating in divine services and receiving sacraments. Whatever references are in the liturgical books that women are unclean and tainted should be abolished. They can enter the Church and receive communion at any time.[19]

More recently, His All-Holiness the Ecumenical Patriarch commissioned a group of scholars to write a document on the social ethos of the Orthodox Church, which was approved by the Holy Synod in 2020. I was honored to be one of the members of this commission. The document that was produced, *For the Life of the Word: Toward a Social Ethos of the Orthodox Church*, states:

> . . . while the Orthodox Church has always held as a matter of doctrine and theology that men and women are equals in personhood, it has not always proved scrupulously faithful to this ideal. The church has, for instance, for far too long retained in her prayers and Eucharistic practices ancient and essentially superstitious prejudices about purity and impurity in regard to women's bodies and has even allowed the idea of ritual impurity to attach itself to childbirth. Yet no Christian woman who has prepared herself for communion through prayer and fasting should be discouraged from approaching the chalice.[20]

The contrast between statements from Antioch and the Ecumenical Patriarchate compared to the Russian Statement on this matter could hardly be greater.

---

18. For a more thorough discussion of the post-Soviet Russian Church's prayer and practices, see my "Matters of Birth and Death."

19. Synod of Antioch, "Announcement," 33.

20. Ecumenical Patriarchate, *For the Life of the World*, ch. 29.

# MENSTRUATION: CHURCH OF OUR GRANDDAUGHTERS

As we have seen, some churches have begun the process of ridding the Orthodox Church of this non-Christian practice that is damaging to all of us. Statements welcoming women at the chalice are excellent, but this message needs to be affirmed by Orthodox bishops and their synods, come from the pulpit, appear in church bulletins, be discussed at coffee hour, be addressed in homes, and so forth. These conversations need to be led by the major clergy, but also by women; women need to have venues in which they can discuss intimate matters of their bodies with other woman in the church.

There is need for sensitivity here. And I'm not seeking to hold the hands of those for whom saying the word "menstruation" at coffee hour will be difficult. If we have been excommunicating women for generations upon generations for this reason, we ought to be able to say (and hear) the word when we reverse the practice. But sensitivity is required because women—in the way that they will always exercise agency and creativity—have made this ban part of their lives. For example, one friend told me that growing up in her large, multigenerational household, the women tended to menstruate at the same time and thus would all stay home from church the same Sunday every month. Essentially, this turned into a big party without the men around for three or four hours! The women cooked and ate breakfast at leisure, swapped stories, did each other's hair—all without any masculine presence. There was a sense of freedom and relief. "Honestly," my friend told me, "we would have been upset if the priest called and said we had to go to church during our periods!" Sensitivity is also necessary because Orthodox faithful may be upset to learn that what they have been taught by their priests and their families is not true.

I love this image of women in a family at leisure together. For families who have created traditions like this, there is a way to educate, to explain there is no theological or practical reason for a ban from the chalice, and to simultaneously respect their own familial culture and allow them to ease into attendance during menstruation as best makes sense to them.

I envision, for example, parish-level conversations taking place in which (female and male) leaders make clear that women and girls are welcome at the chalice. I hope for a church in which the worthiness of women and their bodies is affirmed, and the Incarnation is witnessed in this way. It is my hope and prayer that the only restraints placed on our granddaughters' approach to the chalice are the universal expectations of prayer and fasting. Our Lord Jesus Christ invited us to "come to him." All of our grandchildren, and all the faithful, should be therefore welcomed at the chalice as an affirmation of our incarnational and eucharistic theology.

# 3

# Churching

*I envision all mothers in the church of our granddaughters experiencing Churching as a rite of hospitality and blessing that no longer contains any theologically poor, pastorally harmful, and unChristian connections between birth and impurity and offers male and female children the same ritual treatment.*

My husband and I were the first of our college friends to marry. The Orthodox service took place in my hometown parish in West Virginia and was cause for all manner of remarks. One theme for teasing at the reception was the many references to childbearing in the service; a friend memorably remarked that he was sure he had just witnessed a fertility rite. It is true that multiple petitions are offered for the fruitfulness of a couple's union during an Orthodox marriage service, such as "that He will grant unto them the enjoyment of the blessing of children, . . . let us pray to the Lord." Yet, the primary purpose of marriage in the Orthodox understanding is not childbearing. Instead, it is the sacramental union of the couple who work to secure each other's mutual deification. Childbearing is indeed understood to be a great blessing in marriage and, therefore, this blessing is quite naturally hoped and prayed for within the marriage ceremony.[1]

---

1. All marriages in the Orthodox Church are sacramentally valid whether

There is a ritual for new Orthodox Christian mothers and their babies that marks the occasion the mother first returns to church after childbirth and when the baby first makes an appearance. The presence of these prayers signifies that childbirth is a spiritual experience, deserving of attention by the entire community. This contrasts with the contemporary culture's view of childbirth primarily through a medical lens, with any spiritual component perceived as an optional add-on.[2]

One might assume that the Orthodox prayers said *after* the birth of a child would be full of thanksgiving and rejoicing; the nuptial prayers have, after all, been answered.[3] Instead, these qualities are noticeably lacking from the post-childbirth prayers that are part of the Orthodox *Book of Needs* (or *Euchologion* or *Trebnik*), the compendium of services used by Orthodox priests for services that address the human experience from birth to the grave and beyond. This service book includes Churching, the ritual welcoming mother and baby to church after childbirth, more formally known as "Prayer for a Woman on the Fortieth Day of Childbirth."

What stands out in the Churching prayers is not thankfulness or rejoicing, but the mother's imputed "uncleanness" or "impurity" or "defilement" as a result of childbirth. The concept of childbirth as defiling is not supported by the marriage rite, has no sound theological basis (much like the excommunication during menstruation), and—interestingly—was added to these prayers at a relatively late date.

There is a profound mismatch between the denigration of the female body present in Churching and the Orthodox Church's teachings on the Incarnation, the human body, the value of maternity, and human life in the womb and childbirth. Like the excommunication

---

they include children or not, as affirmed by the words of Saint John Chrysostom, "But suppose there is no child; do they remain two and not one? No; their intercourse effects the joining of their bodies, and they are made one, just as when perfume is mixed with ointment." John Chrysostom, "Homily 12 on Colossians."

2. For a discussion of childbirth's perceived spiritual significance today, see Howard, *Showing*, 12–13.

3. Of course, there are times when childbearing takes place outside of wedlock, and in these cases the Churching of the mother and baby takes place just as it would in the case of a married mother.

of menstruating women and girls, this is a practice that is out of step with the Orthodox Church's own theological truths.

I include this and the following chapter knowing well that not all women will become mothers, nor is it necessary to be a mother to be a good Christian or a good woman. Still, the misbegotten and harmful language in the Churching and miscarriage prayers (discussed in the next chapter) not only demeans women but, in so doing, harms us all—mothers and all women and men because it compromises the Orthodox Church's understanding of the Incarnation and the human body.[4] With participation from both hierarchy and laity, Churching can certainly be altered between now and the time of our granddaughters. In some quarters of the Orthodox Church, this change is already underway.

## CHURCHING: PAST

The first prayer of Churching in use today includes these lines about the mother: "Purify her, therefore, from every sin and from every defilement [often translated as "filth"] as she now draws near to Thy holy church; and let her be counted worthy to partake, uncondemned, of Thy Holy Mysteries."[5]

And the second prayer continues the theme:

> O Lord our God, Who didst come for the salvation of the human race, come also upon Thy servant, *Name*, and count her worthy, through the prayers of Thine honorable Priest, of entrance into the temple of Thy Glory. Wash away her bodily and spiritual uncleanness, in the completion of the forty days. Make her worthy also of the communion of Thy precious Body and Blood.[6]

---

4. For a longer discussion of the history and theology of Churching and the concept of impurity, see my chapter "Postpartum" in *Maternal Body*.

5. "Prayers on the Fortieth Day," *Great Book of Needs*, 10–11. This translation of the Churching prayers is commonly in use in Slavic parishes in the United States, and its rendering of the impurity language is quite similar to other English translations.

6. "Prayers on the Fortieth Day," 12. The period of forty days is modeled on Leviticus regarding how long a woman should refrain from coming to the

The message of the prayers is clear: the new mother is considered impure in body and spirit. This is a tragic disassociation between a mother's body and the goodness of its life-creating work. As seen in the previous chapter, the Christian understanding of impurity is that Jesus Christ shifted concepts of impurity from ritualized ones into the realm of free will: "It is not what goes into the mouth that defiles a person, but it is what comes out of the mouth that defiles" (Matt 15:11). Rephrased to address the topic at hand, we might say, "It's not what comes out of the womb of a woman that defiles, but what comes out of her mouth that defiles." But the Churching prayers contradict Christ's understanding and teachings on impurity.

The oldest extant examples of Churching prayers are from the eighth century and do not include any impurity language.[7] These early prayers are focused entirely on the baby; mention of the mother is absent. These prayers likely functioned as pre-baptismal prayers. Babies were given a proto-Christian sort of status, since unbaptized adults were not allowed to stay for the full liturgy at this time.

Given these examples of early Churching prayers, we can tentatively conclude that there was likely not a continuous ritual of Churching following Mary's purification (Christ's presentation in the temple recorded in Luke 2:22–38) nor following the inauguration of this feast in the fourth century (celebrated on February 2). As best we can tell, it was in the eighth century that a Churching prayer for the baby appeared and mention of the mother, along with concerns of her impurity, was added later, around the twelfth century.[8] There may have been local customs that were not recorded,

---

temple after childbirth (Lev 12:1–7). Interestingly, rather than dictate a longer time for female infants (the eighty days required in Leviticus) than male infants (forty days required in Leviticus), the Churching rite universalizes forty days for both sexes.

7. For more about the late introduction of purity language into Churching and the history and development of Churching in general, see Arranz, "Les Sacrements de Euchologe," 284–302; Streett, "What to Do with the Baby?," 51–71; and Stuhlman, *Initiatory Process*.

8. Additionally, the fourteenth-century "Prayers on the First Day After a Woman Has Given Birth to a Child" that are included in the *Book of Needs*

and the association between impurity and childbirth was certainly present in some cases.[9] The lack of a rite clearly associated with Mary's purification is important because a link to her purification is often how pastors today explain the purity language: "If it was good enough for the Mother of God, it's good enough for you."

Speculation about why the impurity language was added to Churching does not yield one, clear reason. There were likely many factors, including an increased interest in ritual details in the late Byzantine era (practices such as clergy ritually washing hands before preparing the Eucharist, which are still in place today, were added at this time) as well as an apparent development of a very sin-focused and body-denying form of Christian-interpreted Levitical law that was not a simple revival of an ancient Israelite understanding of ritual purity but was instead an intentional association between sin and impurity. A disproportionate degree of attention was given to women's bodies within this way of thinking. Notably, this was also the era in which the ordained order of deaconesses ceased to exist in the East, partly on the premise that the putative impurity of menstruation excludes women from the altar. Some scholars have suggested the possible influence of the Christian West via the Fourth Crusade, which, drawing on an Augustinian notion of original sin, had included impurity in its prayers at an earlier time. Whatever the influences or motivations, the introduction of impurity into the Orthodox Churching prayer was a later Byzantine innovation.

Another matter of concern with Churching is ritual action involving the baby. A Russian friend of mine once told me that when she arrived early for Liturgy and saw a Churching of an infant taking place, the sure tip-off as to the sex of the baby was whether the priest carried the baby around the altar (for a boy) or did not (for a girl). Contrary to the rubrics about Churching present in some

---

(and intended to be said by the priest on the day after childbirth) were added to the service books well after the Churching prayers. The "First Day" prayers contain the putative link between childbirth and impurity from its earliest textual examples.

9. See Afentoulidou's comments on this subject in her review of my book *Maternal Body*, 100.

*Book of Needs* today,[10] this tradition has a mixed history; there are examples of both sexes being carried around the altar, neither sex being carried around the altar, and—as in my Russian friend's story—only males carried around the altar.[11] As Robert Taft writes, "the earliest manuscripts of the rite do not preclude the introduction of a female child into the sanctuary during the Churching."[12] The fact that there is no justifiable theological or pastoral reason for carrying only male babies around the altar combined with the variety of practices in the Orthodox past makes a strong case for the same treatment of the sexes in this part of the Churching rite—with either or neither sex making the trip around the altar.

## CHURCHING: TODAY

The language of impurity falls hard on a new mother's ears—and the ears of her husband and the rest of the parish. While past generations might have been more accepting of the perceived authority of the prayer book, today the faithful rightly recognize the association between childbirth and impurity as in jarring contradiction to everything else they have been taught about Christian family life and the holiness of the human body.

This language also rings harshly precisely because of the Christian understanding of impurity as sin. When we implore the Spirit to "cleanse us from every impurity," in the Trisagion prayers used in every service, we are not referring to, for example, washing ourselves of the ritual taint acquired by eating an animal killed by another animal (Lev 17:15); we are asking for remission of our sins. For new parents to be told that the mother is "unclean" because she just gave birth is not only inaccurate, but confusing and damaging.

Additionally, the forty-day period between childbirth and Churching is another example of excommunication, similar to the

---

10. "Prayers on the Fortieth Day," 15.

11. See Robert Taft's comments about the sexes in the altar during Churching in "Women at Church," 79, as well as Matthew Street's discussion of the same in "What to Do with the Baby?," 70.

12. Taft, "Women at Church," 79.

menstruation excommunication discussed in chapter 1. The new mother is effectively banned from church, and therefore the chalice, until her Churching (the forty days is not strictly observed in many places; it may be more, it may be less). It is highly unusual for a priest to bring her communion while at home recovering from childbirth, which is exactly what a priest might do in any other shut-in situation (in the case of an elderly person or someone who is ill). There is inherent wisdom and sense in giving woman a blessing to stay home after childbirth because this is a time when rest and recovery are needed. It is also unique and helpful in Orthodox practice that the language around forgiveness in Churching can be understood as sanction for the woman to return to the Eucharist without going to confession first, which is striking because typically there is an expectation that someone who experiences a long absence for any reason will go to confession before receiving communion.[13] This is a mercy; mothers have many competing demands on their time in the postpartum era. However, these are "benefits" of the way the prayers function, not the purpose or reason for the prayers, and these benefits are tarnished by the implicit and functional excommunication of the mother.

It is not just laypeople who are perturbed by the impurity language in the prayers; there is a widespread reluctance among clergy to pray them as they are written. Some Orthodox priests change the language of Churching on the fly—something done with no other liturgical service that I know of. Priests sometimes offer, as mine did with my second child, to say the prayers in a language that the mother does not comprehend and thus sparing her from understanding them. This is truly indicative of something awry, as Orthodox prayers ought to be in the vernacular. Some priests read the Churching prayers as they are, but then have no good explanation of postpartum impurity when asked—because there is not one. At least one Greek translation of the *Book of Needs* softens some of the impurity language, placing the Greek language prayers—impurity and all—on the left-hand page and the English

13. Even though Churching can and, in many instances, does function as a sort of absolution, some parishes today expect or require the woman to go to confession before returning to the Eucharist.

translation—impurity language considerably softened—on the right, with no explanation for this change.

I know of one hierarch who understands the impurity mentioned in these prayers as a sort of impurity acquired after close contact with the holy. In this thinking, the mother's role in the creation of a new human person brings her too close to God and she must be purified in order to re-enter mundane reality. (Interestingly, even with this generous interpretation of impurity, the same hierarch believes the rites ought to be changed because of the pastoral harm they do.) This was also the explanation offered by Father Alexander Schmemann to his female students. It is well intentioned, but ultimately hermeneutical gymnastics; there is no hint of this meaning in the rites or in their history.[14] Not only is this meaning absent from the rites, but it also belies the profound complexity of childbirth. For many women, childbirth is not all sweetness and light. It can be dislocating, disturbing, humiliating, both ecstatic and tortuous, both liberative and oppressive. Any efforts to change the language of these prayers would do well to preserve a certain intensity of language and retain an acknowledgment of the possible ambiguity of the experience.

Sanctioned change is beginning to come to these prayers. The Antiochian Orthodox Church of North America (AOCNA) has published a new volume of initiation services, including Churching as well as Baptism and the reception of converts into the Orthodox Church.[15] All references to impurity in the Churching prayers are placed in parenthesis, so they can be easily omitted.[16]

The Ukrainian Orthodox Church of the USA (UOC) is in the process of printing a new version of Churching in its forthcoming

14. This interpretation raises, but does not examine, all sorts of other theological questions, such as: why don't we all need purification after we receive the Eucharist?

15. Najim and O'Grady, "Service of Churching," 17–31. These changes are explained in an appendix, which notes that the focus on impurity in the *Book of Needs'* postpartum prayers "separates us from the most important pastoral aspect: giving of thanks and glorifying God," "Appendix A," 136.

16. Najim and O'Grady's *Services of Initiation* also includes a version of the miscarriage prayers that lacks the impurity language and addresses other theological problems with these prayers.

baptismal handbook for clergy.[17] This version goes further than the optional omission of impurity language in the Antiochian volume; the new Ukrainian Churching deletes references to impurity altogether. This Churching, developed by a group of women scholars and faithful and printed at the end of this chapter, includes new language of hospitality and welcome.[18] This cooperation between laity and hierarchs may serve as a model for future such projects.

Given the structure of the Orthodox Church, and with the exception of the Churching prayers created for the UOC, most of these changes to the Churching prayers are being made and approved by men—priests in parishes and metropolitan offices, bishops approving translations and new prayer books, and so forth. Their efforts are laudable and very welcome. Yet, it would be most appropriate for theologically trained women who have given birth and then walked back through the narthex doors to rejoin their community with an infant in their arms to recraft the Churching prayers which would then be adopted by bishops. This is not to suggest that the Orthodox Church's male clergy have nothing to offer new mothers, but it is to say that it is fitting for mothers to pen these prayers, given their history and given the fact that mothers understand what the postpartum time period is like in a way that the male clergy simply cannot, no matter how sympathetic, well-intentioned, or pastorally gifted.

The matter of the postpartum rites is unambiguous: impurity is not part of the church's understanding of childbirth or women's bodies. These rites could be replaced or altered by all jurisdictions, not just the AOCNA or UOC, with relative ease and with the willing assistance of Orthodox mothers. Orthodox synods could easily call upon women/mother scholars to craft new Churching rites and then distribute them.

---

17. Ukrainian Orthodox Church of the USA, *Initiation*, forthcoming, 2023.

18. This group included Sasha Safchuk, Valerie Zahirsky, Mary Ann De-Trana, me, and, may their memories be eternal, Stefanie Yazghe and Daria Petrykowski.

## CHURCHING: CHURCH OF
## OUR GRANDDAUGHTERS

I envision continued work on the revision of Churching, revision that is directed by women and especially mothers along with the approval and dissemination by hierarchs. Deep awareness of how these prayers are explained by women and how they have been passed down will inform this work.[19] Although different Orthodox jurisdictions or churches are free to adopt the work of others, it is also acceptable in terms of our liturgical history for many Churching rites to come into existence; there are many ways to mark the occasion of mother and baby coming to church after childbirth that honor the mothers and babies in harmony with the Orthodox Church's incarnational theology. Also, churches may approach differently the inconsistency between male and female babies going around the altar; some may decide to direct the priest to carry both sexes behind the altar, others may omit this part of the service, and still others may give the option to do one or the other, with both sexes treated the same. The Orthodox Church of Finland recently decided that neither male nor female babies should be carried into the altar during Churching.[20]

Other matters call for attention, too. The role of the father and the godparents deserves consideration, especially given that Churching is a pre-baptismal rite for the baby (and godparents are very much a part of the baptism rite). Adoption of children does not always take place during infancy, which means that much of the language of Churching does not make sense in this context. New versions of the Churching prayers should be developed to minister to the welcome of children to a family by way of adoption and fostering.

With women and especially mothers composing revised prayers for Churching, these prayers will authentically reflect the church's long-standing esteem for mothers, childbirth, the human person, and the human body. These prayers will then include all

19. See, e.g., Kalkun, "How to Ask Embarrassing Questions," 97–115.
20. Kupari and Voula, *Orthodox Christianity and Gender*, 1.

the things that mothers ought to hear from the church when they return to their community for the first time after childbirth—from welcome, to praise, to celebration of birthgiving and new life, to thanksgiving for having endured pregnancy and childbirth, to preservation of both mother and child, to beseeching strength and wisdom for the days of motherhood to come.

There is great value in marking a mother's return to church for the first time after childbirth and welcoming her baby into the community. The Churching prayers are in need of revision, not excision. In the hands of the church's mother-theologians, I envision our granddaughters (whether mothers themselves or witnesses to the rite) experiencing the Churching prayers as rightly celebrating motherhood and the presence of a new human being. It is my hope that in the church of our granddaughters, there will be consistency and continuity between the joyful anticipation of children within the marriage rite and joyful welcome for mother and baby in the Churching prayers.

## PRAYERS FOR THE MOTHER
## OF THE CHILD[21]

O Lord our God, Who came for the salvation of the human race, come also upon Your servant, N., and receive her through the prayers of Your honorable Priest, into the temple of Your glory. She comes in the footsteps of the Theotokos and generations of other mothers. Forgive her any sin she may have committed these forty days and make her worthy of the communion of Your precious Body and Blood. May she know your mercy and compassion in all her days of motherhood and share these things with her child, for sanctified and glorified is Your most honorable and majestic Name, of the Father and of the Son, and of the Holy Spirit, now and ever and unto ages of ages. Amen.

21. Excerpted from "Prayers for a Woman on the Fortieth Day of Childbirth," *Initiation*, Ukrainian Orthodox Church of USA, forthcoming 2023.

O God the Father Almighty, You foretold by Your mighty-voiced Prophet Isaiah of the Incarnation from a Virgin of Your Only-begotten Son and our God, and You deigned to become an infant of her, by Your good pleasure and cooperation of the Holy Spirit, for our salvation, and through Your immeasurable loving-kindness. According to the custom of Your holy Law, You were brought into the Sanctuary after the fulfillment of the days of purification, being Yourself the true Lawgiver and the fulfiller of the Law, and you were carried in the arms of righteous Simeon, praised by the Prophetess Anna, and, echoing the aforementioned Prophet, you were revealed like the coal in the tongs. O Lord Who guards infants and who we the faithful have an imitation by Grace, bless this child, together with his (her) parents and his (her) sponsors, and count him (her) worthy, in due season, of the new birth through water and the Spirit; number him (her) with Your holy flock of rational sheep, who are called by the name of Your Christ. For You dwell on high, and regard the lowly, and unto You we send up glory, to the Father, and to the Son, and to the Holy Spirit, now and ever, and unto the ages of ages.

# 4

# Miscarriage

*I envision women who experience miscarriage, stillbirth, or the death of a newborn receiving compassionate pastoral care from the Orthodox Church in the church of our granddaughters— care that is reflective of the unique grief experienced when a precious and irreplaceable soul is so briefly known, including prayers and services that offer comfort and hope in the resurrection and the life to come.*

My oldest brother was stillborn, at nearly full term. He was my parents' first child, and I can only begin to comprehend how heartbroken they were. My mother kept photos of him in her nightstand until she died, and then I took careful possession of those pictures, which I still look at from time to time. After his birth, my mother called the priest from the hospital. The priest said, "There is nothing I can do for you." He didn't visit my parents in the hospital, he didn't visit them at home, he certainly did not oversee the burial of my brother's tiny body. This kept my mother away from the Orthodox Church for decades. She had grown up, by her own account, in a "hellfire and brimstone" Southern Baptist family and stopped going to church the day she turned eighteen. She married my Orthodox father with the blessing of the bishop and had been warming to Orthodoxy, but this sad experience with her firstborn cooled things.

Two decades (and three parish priests) later, she converted to Orthodoxy and became one of the most devout and Christ-radiant people I have ever known.

When the priest who told her that there was "nothing he could do" retired, he called my mother. He told her that his words to her were one of the greatest regrets of his priesthood. He asked for her forgiveness, and she freely gave it. This was a moment of profound healing and grace for them both.

There are counter stories of priests providing compassionate comfort to mothers (and fathers) in situations of miscarriage and stillbirth, to be sure, but there are also many instances of neglect, pain, disappointment brought about by the Orthodox Church at these times (as seen in my mother's story). And these situations are not few in number. Considering that a quarter of women are thought to experience miscarriage in their lifetimes and that even the developed world is not immune from stillbirth and the death of newborns, it is clear that a large percentage of Orthodox Christians are touched by these events.

Failing to provide compassionate pastoral care in times of miscarriage is a failure to live out the understanding that God is present at all times and that through death comes resurrection, comes new life. These bereavements cannot be "fixed" with hope in Christ, but there are Orthodox methods and ways of ministering to those who are bereaved by these particular losses, and the Orthodox Church ought never add to their pain.

It is not just that Orthodox priests may say the "wrong thing" or fail to attend to their bereaved parishioners in these situations, it is also that the prayers provided by the Orthodox Church—similar to the Churching prayers—are deeply flawed and pastorally damaging. *The Book of Needs* includes "Prayer for a Woman When She has Miscarried/Aborted an Infant." This prayer holds the mother as culpable for any loss of life in the womb and conflates unintentional pregnancy loss (miscarriage) with abortion. "Have mercy on this Thy handmaid who today is in sin, having fallen into *the killing of a person*, whether voluntary or involuntary, and has cast out that conceived in her"[1] (italics not my own). This is not a problem of translation. Though translations into English naturally vary, the culpability is present in the Greek and Church Slavonic. As much as I wish my parents had been ministered to by the Orthodox Church, I am so glad my mother was spared from hearing a priest charge her with "killing" her own son as she recovered from the pregnancy and delivery of her dead firstborn. And yet, many women in the Orthodox Church have suffered exactly this experience.

Not all women will be mothers, and not all of our granddaughters will be mothers. Just as in the case of Churching explored in the last chapter, however, how we treat miscarriage has consequences not isolated to mothers—there are consequences for the entire community because our understanding of who we are as human beings is at stake. Here is another chasm between the theological truths of Orthodox theology and its practices when it comes to women. But this chasm is readily bridgeable; the Orthodox Church has ample resources, including its appreciation for human life, women, motherhood, and childbearing, as well as its understanding of death. We are capable of ministering to miscarriage and stillbirth—and repentance after abortion—in a loving, compassionate, and Christian fashion. This is my hope for the church of our granddaughters.

## MISCARRIAGE: PAST

The "Prayer for a Woman When She has Miscarried/Aborted an Infant" appears to have been first added to the compendiums of the church in about the fifteenth century but was not widely (and still not universally) included in prayer books until the seventeenth century. (Note that it postdates the inclusion of purity language in Churching addressed in the previous chapter.)[2] In the Orthodox context, with many rites easily traced back twelve hundred years, these prayers are relatively young. The rubrics in a popular English

---

1. "Prayer for a Woman Miscarried/Aborted," *Great Book of Needs*, 16–18.

2. Glibetić, "Orthodox Liturgical Rites," 160. For more information about the history of the miscarriage rite, see both Glibetić and Afentoulidou, "Childbed Prayers."

translation used in the United States dictate "forty days of purifica-tion . . . after the unfortunate occurrence,"[3] which, like the forty days before Churching, is another form of excommunication for women based on circumstance, not sin. (See chapter 2 for a discus-sion of excommunication and Churching.)

The slash between "Miscarried" and "Aborted" in the title of the rite might suggest that two different rites are included: one for unintended pregnancy loss (miscarriage and stillbirth) and the other for cases of deliberate and intended pregnancy loss (abor-tion). This is not the case; it is meant for both occasions and, to a large degree, these two occasions are conflated in the rite. The rite contains one long prayer, which includes two repetitions of the line previously quoted: "Have mercy on this Thy handmaid who today is in sin, having fallen into *the killing of a person*, whether volun-tary or involuntary, and has cast out that conceived in her."[4] A bit of a distinction is heard between "involuntary murder," meaning miscarriage, and "voluntary murder," meaning abortion. But the woman is equally culpable for both, and they are both considered "murder."

The most generous interpretation of the language around voluntary and involuntary "murder" and pregnancy loss is that it may have resulted from the fact that throughout human history most cultures held any number of often incorrect beliefs about how woman might purposefully or inadvertently lose a pregnancy: eating certain foods, lifting heavy objects, running, etc.[5] My oldest child was born in the first year of the new millennium when I was living in the rural United States, and I was told many times that I could lose the pregnancy by lifting my arms over my head, such as I might do when placing sweaters on a high shelf in a closet. These

3. "Prayer for a Woman Miscarried/Aborted," 16.

4. "Prayer for a Woman Miscarried/Aborted," 16. The prayers also include some putative association with childbearing and impurity, which I have cov-ered in chapter 2.

5. See Glibetić's history of the rite for a discussion of the possible influence of "unsanctioned ritual responses"—meaning non-Christian magical spells and totems of the era—which might have prompted the creation of such rite as a sanctioned alternative. "Orthodox Liturgical Rites," 166–71.

sorts of persistent misperceptions, superstitions, and speculations about causes for pregnancy loss may have elicited uncharitable suspicion regarding the mother's motives. The personal narrative of the woman herself was clearly not to be believed by the church. She was blamed and held responsible for any miscarriage as though it were intentional. The miscarriage prayers are focused on assigning guilt rather than providing consolation.

In the circumstance of intended abortion, "Prayer for a Woman When She Has Miscarried/Aborted an Infant" takes on a different light. Here these prayers appear to provide a means of reconciliation with the church after an abortion. The hope for healing and protection for the mother is heard: "Heal her suffering, and grant her with a shining angel from every assault of invisible demons; yea, O Lord, from sickness and weakness . . . by Thine abundant mercy, rouse her humbled body, and raise her up from the bed on which she lies. . . ."[6] The associated rubrics make suggestions, but not demands, that the priest direct the woman to penance and possibly prohibit her from receiving communion for a limited period of time, anticipating her return to the chalice. There is an implicit and compassionate acknowledgment here of the many unhappy circumstances that lead women to abortion. Paradoxically, the prayer is more compassionate to women who had an abortion than women who had a miscarriage.

The Orthodox Church continues to address these topics. Recent social statements from both the Russian Orthodox Church and the Ecumenical Patriarchate both unequivocally condemn the act of abortion, and both documents provide canonical, scriptural, and other references to support the long history of the Christian appreciation that, as *For the Life of the Word: Toward a Social Ethos of the Orthodox Church* (the document from the Ecumenical Patriarchate) phrases it, "a child's claim upon our moral regard then is absolute from that first moment, and Christians are forbidden from shedding innocent blood at every stage of human development."[7] In the words of the Russian *Basis of the Social Concept*:

---

6. "Prayer for a Woman Miscarried/Aborted," 16.

7. Ecumenical Patriarch, *For the Life of the World*, ch. 25.

Since the ancient time the church has viewed deliberate abortion as a grave sin. The canons equate abortion with murder. This assessment is based on the conviction that the conception of a human being is a gift of God. Therefore, from the moment of conception any encroachment on the life of a future human being is criminal.[8]

Notably, both documents provide for the extreme case of abortion when the mother's life is at risk, and both documents reference reconciliation with the church after an abortion. The "Prayer for a Woman When She Has Miscarried/Aborted an Infant" may be a ritual means for this. To what extent it is being used as such today is not clear (this is an understudied phenomenon and complicated by the fact that these prayers have fallen out of use in the case of miscarriage in much of North America and Europe).[9] The compassionate response to situations of abortion is notably divergent from the Russian Orthodox Church's excommunication from the Eucharist during menstruation, as discussed in chapter 1, and is striking in comparison to the general lack of compassion for miscarriage from the Orthodox Church.[10]

## MISCARRIAGE: TODAY

In the twenty-first century, some causes of miscarriage are known: chromosomal problems; toxins in the environment; problems with the placenta, cervix, or uterus; or problems with the father's sperm. Yet, sometimes a miscarriage has no obvious explanation. The woman is not guilty in any of these circumstances.

The Orthodox miscarriage prayers ought to be changed to reflect this knowledge, and to provide comfort, not further distress, to the bereaved woman (as well as to her husband, their other children, godparents, etc.). Some women who experience miscarriage

8. Russian Orthodox Church, *Basis of the Social Concept*, XII.2.

9. In Russia, for example, akathists (special hymns dedicated to a saint or event) for penitent women who have had an abortion are available online and in popular use but are not church-sanctioned. See Kizenko, "Feminized Patriarchy?," 599.

10. Russian Orthodox Church, "On Participation of the Faithful."

have feelings of guilt, even though they are not at fault. However, there are ways to pray for a woman's unwarranted feelings of guilt or responsibility without labeling her as a "murderess." It has been argued that in its original, late-Byzantine setting, this rite revealed the concern of the clergy, as Nina Glibetić characterizes it, to "enter into domestic spaces in order to affirm God's mercy specifically to women who suffer,"[11] but in its contemporary, twenty-first-century context, this rite intensifies suffering in its hubristic and insensitive assertions of the mother's culpability.

In response to the many failings of this rite and the Orthodox Church's poor pastoral care of miscarriage, stillbirth, and pregnancy loss, some churches are seeking to change. Many priests alter this rite on the fly, or pencil in annotations in their copies of the *Book of Needs*, much like Churching. While this is helpful, this rite needs systematic review and alteration.

The Orthodox Church in America (OCA) contributed to the consolation of many when its Synod approved a "Service after Miscarriage or Stillbirth" in 2015, which can be found online and is used both within and outside the OCA.[12] It is notable that this service was composed and approved largely through the efforts of a woman who cared very deeply about these situations. Orthodox Christian Dennise Krause worked for years to see this rite come to fruition. The "Service after Miscarriage or Stillbirth" is comprised of litanies for the departed interspersed with prayers; somewhat like a litya, a memorial service for the departed. Several lines comfort the parents: "For the servants of God, [NN.], who have suffered the repose of a child during pregnancy, and for their family and friends, that they may be comforted, let us pray to the Lord." Others attend to the lost life: "That He will receive the infant [N.], who by His ineffable providence has been taken from his/her mother's womb and will grant him/her life everlasting, let us pray to the Lord."[13] Krause also created several accompanying materials, such as a guide for experiencing this bereavement and pastoral guides

---

11. Glibetić, "Orthodox Liturgical Rites," 179.

12. Orthodox Church in America, "Service after Miscarriage or Stillbirth."

13. Orthodox Church in America, "Service after Miscarriage or Stillbirth."

for priests to increase their skills in assisting these situations, much of which remains unpublished.

In addition to this work in the OCA, the Antiochian Orthodox Church of North America (AOCNA) has also taken steps. A recent Antiochian volume of initiation services (mentioned regarding Churching prayers in the previous chapter) includes a newly translated ancient prayer for situations of miscarriage that omits any implication that the mother may have caused the death of the life she was carrying.[14]

A few books on topics such as miscarriage, pregnancy loss, and infertility written by Orthodox women have appeared in recent years, such as Jenny Schrodel's *Naming the Child: Hope-filled Reflections on Miscarriage, Stillbirth, and Infant Death* and Nicole Roccas's *Under the Laurel Tree: Grieving Infertility with Saints Joachim and Anna.* Recent Orthodox-authored books treating topics of pregnancy and childbearing often include a chapter or an appendix that addresses this bereavement, including Laura S. Jansson's *Fertile Ground: A Pilgrimage through Pregnancy* and Sarah Bragwynne and Sasha Rose Oxnard's *A Sacred Beginning: Nurturing Your Body, Mind, and Soul during Baby's First Forty Days.*[15] These are welcome additions to the Orthodox understanding of these topics.

One of the reasons that reform of these prayers is so important is that Orthodox priests rely on church-vetted, formal prayers for any occasion; ours is not a tradition in which freestyling prayer is common or comfortable (at least for the clergy). In some cases, priests have the good sense to refrain from using "Prayer for a Woman When She has Miscarried/Aborted an Infant," but the

14. The editors of *Services of Initiation* leave this footnote: "If it is determined, however, that any voluntary motive attaches here, the priest must guide the woman to contrition, holy Confession and repentance according to the sacred canons." It seems that the priest, not the woman, is still the final arbiter in judgment of the status of the miscarriage as voluntary or involuntary, an unfortunate continuation of the mistrust and disenfranchisement of women from the more ancient miscarriage rite. Najim and O'Grady, *Services of Initiation*, 27n19.

15. Jansson, "Appendix: Losing a Baby," in *Fertile Ground*, 307–11, and Bragwynne and Oxnard, "Loss," in Bragwynne and Oxnard, *Sacred Beginning*, 362–65.

result too often is that *no* comfort or pastoral support is offered. I suspect many women do not tell their priest about miscarriage, out of shame and discomfort, or even doubt that the priest might be a source of solace. Both reform of the rite and pastoral training to better minister to such loss are needed in the Orthodox Church. The dismal status of pastoral care for women in these situations also points to the need for the reinstatement of ordained deaconesses in the Orthodox Church so that, appropriately, women may minister to women and their families in these situations, discussed in more detail in chapter 6.

Funeral or memorial services are also needed to minister well to such loss. "The Order for the Burial of an Infant" in the *Book of Needs* addresses the death of a baptized infant or child, defined as up to seven years old. The primary difference between this rite and the one available for adult laypersons is that the child in question is considered unstained by sin; there is a noticeable absence of prayers for forgiveness in "The Order for the Burial of an Infant." Yet, there is no funeral rite for cases of miscarriage, stillbirth, or the fleeting life of a born but unbaptized infant—the human persons who are most clearly without the need for remissions of sins.[16] For a community that so greatly values human life at all stages in the womb, this is a serious and unnecessary lacuna. Recognizing the need, some priests use the "The Order for the Burial of an Infant" for persons who were miscarried or stillborn or dead before they could be baptized. Other priests alter this rite for these situations. There are also proposed additional rites (such as memorial services) specific to pregnancy loss and infant death that are circulating among the clergy and faithful, including the unpublished work of Denise Kraus.[17] Additionally, the Russian Orthodox Synod approved a funeral service in 2018 for unbaptized infants, which addresses the

16. A related matter is the inconsistent hospital policies in the United States on the right to take home the miscarried infant's remains. This is a place where the Orthodox Church would do well to advocate.

17. Kraus reports that the Funeral Service she compiled is based on an outline from Fr. Paul Lazor and Fr. Tom Hopko, combined with prayers from other priests. This funeral service has been blessed by Archbishop Michael for use in the New York/New Jersey deanery of the OCA as of 2015. Personal correspondence with Dennis Krause, 2015.

circumstances of stillbirth and infant death (but not miscarriage).[18] To my knowledge, this service has not been translated into English or other languages and remains used only in the Russian context.

In most cases in the Orthodox world, however, there are no funeral and burial rites available. This reveals some discomfort within the Orthodox Church about the status of the unborn. As the press secretary describing the newly created Russian funeral service observed: "The theological understanding of the state of the soul of the deceased infant is not completely determined, there are different points of view regarding this issue."[19] An Assembly of Bishops draft document on "Perinatal and Infant Loss"—which was never, to my knowledge, approved and circulated—suggests that, "although we do not pray for the souls of the unborn as we do for those who are born and then die; the grief of the parents continues."[20] It is true that prayers for miscarriage and stillbirth require different language and should not be the same as for situations of born children who die. Yet, lack of clarity around the status of the person in the womb is not an excuse for telling a woman, "There is nothing I can do for you." Sadly, the need for such rites continues to go largely unaddressed. Furthermore, this fuzziness around the status of the unborn is out of step with the Orthodox conviction of full human personhood in the womb; it is wrong for the Orthodox Church to prize fetal life when it comes to discussions of abortion, but dither about fetal life when it comes to pregnancy loss.

At the same time, Orthodox Christians communally pray about babes in the womb in the liturgy of Saint Basil ("Remember, O God, all those whom we have not remembered through ignorance, forgetfulness or because of their multitude since You know the name and age of each, even from their mother's womb")[21] and regularly advocate for the preservation of life in the womb, and yet there is no designated funeral service for miscarriage, stillbirth, or infant death. In comparison, adult catechumens—who have

18. Russian Orthodox Church, "Unbaptized Infants Allowed Funeral."

19. Russian Orthodox Church, "Unbaptized Infants Allowed Funeral."

20. Assembly of Bishops, "Perinatal and Infant Loss." Also see my discussion of this document in "Pastoral Care of Perinatal."

21. Greek Orthodox Archdiocese of America, "Liturgy of Saint Basil."

expressed their intent to convert to Orthodoxy—are typically given the full adult Orthodox funeral, should they die in their catechumenate, without baptism or chrismation. Surely, infants of Orthodox parents who did not live to see their own birth should be accorded the same status.

We ought to give the unborn their due: Orthodox rites should recognize them as fully human, loved and known by God. The language in such rites will be different than language that addresses the death of a child or an adult, but, ultimately, either the unborn are fully human (as the Orthodox have always held in their convictions about abortion and infant death)—each unique, eternal, and irreplaceable—or they are not.

The situations of miscarriage, stillbirth, and infant loss clearly call for replacement and new services, ideally—as supported in the previous chapter regarding Churching—developed by women themselves. The use of these rites ought to be blessed by bishops, included in pastoral guides, and given as an option for priests and parishioners to consider together. This would be one way to better minister to the bereaved in these situations, and it would simultaneously affirm that a human person—whole and in the image of God—is fashioned in the womb.

## MISCARRIAGE: CHURCH OF OUR GRANDDAUGHTERS

For our granddaughters, I first hope that medical technology continues to advance in such a way as to prevent many miscarriages, stillbirths, and infant deaths. This is already happening, for example, as the understanding of the female reproductive cycle deepened such simple interventions as supplemental hormones in early pregnancy have decreased the rate of miscarriages and the detection and treatment of preeclampsia have decreased the rate of stillbirths.

Furthermore, I envision the Orthodox Church developing rites for situations of miscarriage, stillbirth, and infant death that offer comfort and healing to all involved. Orthodox Christians understand themselves and their world through the liturgy, so it is imperative for the liturgical commemoration of these loses to accurately reflect Orthodox understandings of the human person. As in the case of Churching, cross-jurisdictional or cross-church conformity is not necessary (although different parts of the Orthodox Church ought to be welcome to use rites developed by others); there are many ways to pray in a pastorally sound manner for these situations of loss. Perhaps a version of "Prayer for a Woman When She Has Miscarried/Aborted an Infant" could be kept, renamed, and used for situations in which a women has had an abortion (perhaps also including the father), offering a path of mercy and reconciliation.

Along with considering liturgical needs for all these situations, I envision the Orthodox Church as better educating its pastors to minister compassionately both in seminary and through continuing education. A vital part of this ministry will be including those who are best equipped for it—women—into the minor orders and the ordained diaconate (see chapter 5 and 6). In addition to reforming the Churching and miscarriage rites, Orthodox women should have space to create new rituals that mark women's lives and integrate them into the life of the church. Women as well as men ought to shape the ritual and liturgical future of the Orthodox Church.[22]

For the church of our granddaughters, I hope all women (and their families) who experience this loss will be comforted and guided by excellent pastoral care and comforting prayers for miscarriage, stillbirth, and infant death, and that, thus, the entire community will be assured of the church's consistent and unwavering conviction of the value of human life at all stages and the power of God's mercy to heal.

---

22. For a different perspective and interesting discussion of the possibilities of reforming existing rites and creating new ones to better minister to women, see Ochs, *Inventing Jewish Ritual.*

# 5

# Leadership

*I envision women welcomed and engaged in every level and
aspect of Orthodox Church governance and administration
in the church of our granddaughters. This includes women
abundantly present and involved in the day-to-day leadership of
the church, planning for its future alongside hierarchs, and with
women populating the minor orders; tonsured by the hierarchy
into such ministries as subdeaconess, reader, and cantor.*

Several years ago, the autocephalous Orthodox churches organized
to meet in a council, which had not been attempted for over a
millennium. The planning began nearly a century before, and the
agenda was under discussion for more than six decades. The goal
was to address issues of importance in our contemporary world.

The Holy and Great Council was finally held in Crete in 2016,
composed almost exclusively of (male) Orthodox hierarchs. Four
women were included as non-voting special consultants,[1] with extremely limited opportunities to contribute. They were token repre-
sentatives of their sex in a sea of black-robed and bearded men. In
fact, only at the last minute were women included at all, and only

---

1. Holy and Great Council of the Orthodox Church, "Organization and
Working Procedure," section 3.2, allowed for laity to be appointed as special
consultants.

two out of the ten autocephalous churches that attended the council included women in their official delegations (though women were otherwise present as translators and members of the press).[2] Yet all the issues under review related directly to the lives of women.

This illustrates just how disenfranchised women are within the Orthodox Church. While women are routinely celebrated and appreciated in the larger culture for their skills and accomplishments and some women, in some settings, are joining the ranks of church leadership, women are still more often overlooked, ignored, and diminished. Excluding women from contributing to the leadership and governance of the Orthodox Church not only is bad for women, but it also prevents it from flourishing. It is detrimental and nonsensical for the Orthodox Church to confine itself to, as in the example of the recent council, celibate men to address contemporary social issues such as marriage, divorce, fasting, and so on.

This chapter will explore the roles of women as contributors and leaders in the Orthodox Church in terms of conciliar (council) participation, governance, the minor orders (the related topic of ordained ministry in the Orthodox Church will be reserved for the following chapter), and it will explore the prospect of girls serving in the altar. The discussion of women's leadership that follows also includes exceptional examples of women leaders in the history of the church from which we can learn and be inspired. Women are joining the ranks of church leadership today in significant numbers, but the Orthodox Church continues to limit women's participation in Orthodox life and leadership.

2. I applaud the wisdom of the two hierarchs who included women as special consultants: His All-Holiness, Bartholomew I, Archbishop of Constantinople, New Rome, and Ecumenical Patriarch; and His Beatitude, Anastasios, Archbishop of Tirana, Durrës and All Albania. I also applaud the courage of the four women who were present at the Holy and Great Council as special consultants: Sister Theoxeni, Abbess of the Holy Patriarchal and Stavropegic Monastery of the Life-Giving Spring (Constantinople); Dr. Elizabeth Prodromou, USA (Constantinople); Mother Rakela Dervishi (Albania), Skete of the Myrrh-Bearing Women; and Ms. Sonila Rëmbeci (Albania).

## LEADERSHIP: PAST

The Orthodox Church has a long history of women in leadership and authority even if it has only inconsistently honored this legacy.

The myrrh-bearing women, and particularly Saint Mary Magdalene, are the preeminent woman leaders in the Gospels. All four Gospels report that a group of women disciples went to Jesus Christ's tomb and were the first witnesses to his Resurrection. This act of loyalty, devotion, and witness led the church to refer to them as "apostles to the apostles." The early church is full of examples of women evangelizing and sustaining the burgeoning Christian community. And yet, it appears that Jesus Christ chose only men as apostles. Theologians have wrestled with this seeming contradiction. Greek theologian Konstantinos N. Yokarinis offers a cultural explanation: "Calling women to a preaching role at that time would have overthrown the social order, thus taking on precisely the sort of worldly role that Jesus had rejected by saying his kingdom is 'not of this world' (Matt 22:21)."[3]

Mary, the mother of Jesus, is unparalleled in terms of leadership. The Annunciation is not understood as something imposed upon Mary, but rather as a cooperative act of her will along with God's. She was an active agent in the unfolding plan for Jesus Christ to enter the world when she assented, "Here I am, the servant of the Lord; let it be with me according to your word" (Luke 1:38). In Orthodox tradition Mary, a woman, is understood as a model for all human beings precisely because of this cooperative act of her will. In the words of Elizabeth Behr-Sigel:

> Mary is neither a guardian goddess nor the model for women. Theologians and simple faithful contemplate in her the vision of the new humanity. She is the archetype and guide of those men and women who aspire to give birth to Christ in their hearts and who ask her to intercede for them and to call down upon them the gift of the Spirit.[4]

---

3. Theokritoff, "Gender or Genderlessness of Christ," 24.

4. Behr-Sigel, *Ministry of Women*, 207.

The story of Jesus and the Samaritan woman (told in John 4:1–42), who is revered as Saint Photini in the Orthodox Church, illustrates the unequivocal sanction of women's leadership by Jesus Christ, despite the surprise of his male disciples. Photini and Jesus participate in a long discussion before Photini becomes one of the first evangelists: "Many Samaritans of that town believed in him because of the woman's testimony" (John 4:39). Photini is an early example of a Christian woman who is an evangelist and teacher.

Women were integral to the life and success of the nascent Christian community. The letters of Apostle Paul contain abundant references to women and acknowledge his indebtedness to them,[5] such as Prisca in the letter to the Romans: "Greet Prisca and Aquila, my coworkers in Christ Jesus, who risked their necks for my life, to whom not only I give thanks but also all the churches of the gentiles. Greet also the church in their house" (Rom 16:1–5). Prisca, or Priscilla, is only one example of the many women cited as supporters and benefactors of the church, either in the New Testament or elsewhere, and their philanthropic and financial support of the early church cannot be underestimated.[6] As saints began to be venerated—both monastic and lay saints—women were common among their ranks.

The emphasis in the early church on consecrated virginity and later monasticism opened up new opportunities for women. This mode of life gave women their first socially respectable alternative to life as a homemaker, wife, and mother. With the institutionalization of monastic communities came women leaders in the form of monastery abbesses. (At the same time, it is important to note, there was often a denigration of biological family and of women in these same monastic settings.)[7] For the first twelve hundred years of the church, ordained deaconesses were part of the major orders of clergy (see the next chapter). As scholars Leanne M. Dzubinski and

5. For a discussion of women around the Apostle Paul and the ways their significance has been obscured, see Peppard, "Household Names."

6. See Clark, "Patrons, Not Priests," 253–73.

7. For a discussion of this, and of the way such common language to describe the celibate desert dwellers as "Father" and "Mother" diminishes biological ties and therefore diminishes women, see Wheeler, *Desert Daughters*.

Anneke H. Stasson state, "Women in ministry was not a new idea of the twentieth century as part of 1960s second-wave feminism but was instead God's good plan from the beginning."[8]

Although the ministry and leadership of women was part of "God's good plan," and there are helpful and inspiring examples of women leaders from the early church, women ministering and leading has been rare in the Orthodox Church. As the Orthodox Church institutionalized, patriarchal priorities were included in its structures, and women's participation in leadership was further limited. While there is no golden era of the church in which men and women lived in perfectly enlightened and equitably shared leadership, a falling away from early ideals is witnessed; and today we are left with a situation in which women's ability to lead and minister is severely compromised. In the words of scholar Ashley Purpura, "Despite theological claims about the spiritual equality of men and women . . . an exclusively male hierarchical leadership continues to articulate for Orthodoxy Christians what constitutes 'tradition' and the perimeters of Orthodoxy. Only men sign conciliar statements, write canons, and officiate the liturgical sacraments."[9]

## LEADERSHIP: TODAY

Though the ability of women to lead and participate in church life is, and has been, compromised, women in every era and every place have been essential to the life of the church. I had the good fortune to grow up in a community of many faithful Orthodox Christian women. As a young child, I noticed there were more women present than men at any given service. There were only men in the altar, but the men were substantially outnumbered by the women outside the altar. This disproportion is borne out in research today, too.[10]

These women were not only abundantly present, but they were also central to the functioning of the local church community. Every week a group of them came to church and cleaned the whole thing.

8. Dzubinski and Stasson, *Women in the Mission*, ix.

9. Purpura, "Constructing the Patriarchal Woman," 168.

10. Pew Research Center, "Gender Gap in Religion."

After every service, coffee and food was provided and cleaned up by the women of the parish. These actions are holy and vital to the well-being of parish life. These need not be exclusively women's tasks and I would never make an argument that women ought to be confined only to these roles within parish life. I wish to avoid any disparagement of this sort of domestic ministry, which has traditionally been women's work in the church. Instead, we ought to honor the loving care that is involved in the wiping down of the tables and banisters or the washing out of coffee cups, or the buttering of English muffins (of which I ate so very many as a child).

In addition to hospitality roles, women have begun to step into new roles of leadership and service in parish life. Women of my hometown church, to continue my home parish example, now serve as parish council members, something inconceivable during my childhood. We are in a new era in the Orthodox Church in the ways women are beginning, in significant numbers, to contribute to different facets of church life. There are many factors here, and one of them certainly is societal: because different types of education, training, funding, and professional opportunities are available to women outside of the Orthodox Church, women are bringing their skills and experience *inside* their church communities as well. Additionally, the Orthodox Church itself—clergy and laity alike—is becoming more accepting of women taking on certain roles and tasks.

Recently, Patricia Fann Bouteneff—a founder of Axia Woman, a nonprofit "network by, for, and about Orthodox Women, in the service of Christ"[11]—pulled together a list of what she called "invisible women leaders in the Orthodox Church."[12] She assembled the "invisible leaders" list because she wanted the Orthodox community to know not just the history of women in the Orthodox Church, but also about "our present reality." Part of our present reality is that many Orthodox women are doing many things in the Orthodox Church today.

Bouteneff grouped the list by revealing categories that give a sense of the breadth and depth of the ways that women are

---

11. Axia Women, https://www.axiawomen.org.

12. Bouteneff, "Invisible Leaders."

contributing. Here, with her blessing, I share many of her categories with my own additions and commentary.

- *Chaplaincy.* Women who have professional training to work as chaplains in environments such as hospitals, hospices, and jails.

- *Spiritual direction.* Women who serve as guides or companions on the spiritual path for others. This is a deep part of our Orthodox tradition, with abbesses or nuns serving informally as spiritual directors, and now there are accreditation programs for this as a profession or vocation.

- *Church diplomat.* Women who represent the Orthodox Church in intra-Orthodox or ecumenical spheres, such as the World Council of Churches.

- *Administration.* Women who are abbesses of monasteries or leaders of other Orthodox groups, including trustees and directors of seminaries and other nonprofit boards.

- *Parish and diocesan level leadership positions.* Women who serve as parish council members or as metropolitan governing board members.

- *Finance.* Women who serve as treasurers of parish councils, dioceses, or as chief financial officers of Orthodox institutions.

- *Musicians.* Women who are parish choir directors or cantors or have academic appointments related to music.

- *Scholars.* Women in any number of scholarly fields related to the Orthodox Church: theologians, historians, ethicists, art historians, seminary professors, translators, and otherwise.

- *Religious education.* Women who educate others regarding the Orthodox Church, both on the parish level as catechists of children and adults and as authors and speakers.

- *Church artists.* Women who are iconographers, embroiderers, ecclesiastical tailors, graphic designers, and so forth.

- *Activists.* Women who are working to bring about change in the Orthodox Church in order to better build up the body of Christ. These include leaders of such organizations today as

Axia, Saint Catherine's Vision, and Saint Phoebe Center for the Deaconess, and valuable contributions from the recent past, such as the publication of *St. Nina's Quarterly*.

- *Priests' wives*. Women who are married to priests and minister in this capacity, often with a profound pastoral impact on the life of a parish (acknowledging that there is not one, uniform expression of this role).[13]

- *Sisterhoods/women's guilds*. In many Orthodox Churches, groups of women work together to support the functioning of their parish and philanthropic outreach (such as Philoptochos in the Greek Orthodox context).

- *Readers*. Many women read the epistle in the Divine Liturgy, Psalms and prayers in other services, however almost always without a blessing or tonsuring.

Never in history have so many Orthodox women been able to offer so much relevant expertise to the conciliar, synodal, jurisdictional, and parish life of the Orthodox Church. Continuing to integrate the competency, skills, and experiences of these women by bringing them into roles of leadership, governance, and the minor orders would be consistent with the legacy of Orthodoxy, as well as a great service to faithful the world over.

An expansion of women's roles and leadership in the Orthodox Church is happening not only in North American and Western Europe—the focus of Bounteneff's examples and my own experiences—but also in the autocephalous Orthodox Church in Africa, the Alexandrian Patriarchate. Deaconesses were consecrated there in recent years (a complex situation that will be discussed in detail in the following chapter), and there are also other, local roles for women, such as the position of "Ecclesiarch" in Kenya. This position, blessed by a bishop in the altar, was created by the late Kenyan Bishop Gathuna of Nitria for widowed or older laywomen to manage all liturgical items, preparations, altar management, and generally be in charge of the physical space of the church. Additionally,

13. For a discussion of the role of the priest's wife, see Galadza, "The Priest's Wife," 43–52.

an order of "Preacher" was established by Bishop Gathuna. Women preachers were vetted, trained, and blessed to preach homilies to congregations as well as lead services when a priest was not available.[14] These examples of flexible orders of women blessed by the Orthodox Church and created in response to local needs are a reminder—and a model—of the local church's ability to creatively inaugurate orders that serve local needs and honor and integrate the incarnational realities of women in their communities.

There will be many and far-reaching effects of more and more women entering all manner of roles in the Orthodox Church, whether they be in Africa, Germany, Canada, the United States, or elsewhere. These women will give the gifts they have to offer as unique human persons. Also, additionally, because women and men have very different incarnational realities, this means that women will bring those life experiences to the church in meaningful ways. This is a good thing!

## Councils

Women are now eminently qualified to contribute to the governance of the Orthodox Church. Matters taken up by contemporary councils bear directly on women and their lives, so including women in these aspects of ecclesial life will allow the Orthodox Church to better live out its mission. And yet, there is much work to be done to promote and welcome women into the leadership and governance of the Orthodox Church.

Past Orthodox councils were focused on what one might call more "gender-neutral" matters: the nature of Christ, issues of the church calendar, the expression of the Trinity, the understanding of the Holy Spirit, and so on. In comparison, contemporary councils—if the Holy and Great Council of 2016 is any indication—will be concerned with the life of the faithful and the Orthodox Church in the contemporary world. Perhaps past councils would have benefitted from the presence of women—we will never know. However, such councils were held in eras in which all the theologians, historians,

---

14. Thiani, "Missiology Seminary on Women's Ministries."

canonists, etc., necessary for a council were men, in contrast to the abundance of comparably skilled women in the Orthodox Church today.

Some Orthodox churches (both autocephalous and jurisdictions) have included women at their own conciliar events. Recent councils of the Russian Orthodox Church were composed of 10 percent women delegates, both nuns and laywomen.[15] The Orthodox Church in America includes lay delegates, including women, in its All-American Council. Typically, the Greek Orthodox Archdiocese also allows for lay delegates, and therefore women, at both its Clergy-Laity Congress and its Archdiocesan Council.[16] The Ukrainian Orthodox Church of the USA includes the same at its Sobor.[17] Though given the policies around attendees (which focus on bishops, priests, and deacons), men will invariably outnumber women at these synodal events, nevertheless, women delegates have a say and a vote on matters critical to Orthodox life, such as resolutions of all kinds brought before the council and, in the case of the OCA, the election of the head bishop (metropolitan).[18]

A friend's story illustrates both a general disrespect for women in the Orthodox Church and the lack of women's participation in church-wide councils. When she traveled to the Ecumenical Patriarchate in 1995, she was sent to the basement to eat with several other women visitors. The men, including her husband and son, ate together in the upstairs monastic dining room. When she commented to the young monk who led the women downstairs, that she hoped this would change someday, he replied, "It never will." "Why?" she asked. The answer came: "Because women are not on the agenda." Understood figuratively or literally, this needs to change. Women ought to be on the agenda, and composing it.

15. Kizenko, "Feminized Patriarchy?," 598–601.

16. Greek Orthodox Archdiocese of America, "Regulations, 2019," Article VI, Section 5.

17. Ukrainian Orthodox Church of the USA, "XXXII Sobor."

18. Orthodox Church in America, "All-American Council," III.

## Minor Orders

Another area for improvement regarding women in the leadership of the Orthodox Church is in what are often called the "minor orders." Reader, cantor, and subdeacon are the most common minor orders in the contemporary Orthodox Church, though there are other minor orders from Orthodoxy's past that might inform Orthodoxy's future. Essentially, a minor order was a special role in the church community that came with particular responsibilities. I will save the "major orders"—deacon, priest, and bishop—for the next chapter.

While the minor orders in the Orthodox context have been fluid historically, they are considered to stand apart from the major orders because people are *tonsured* into the minor orders, whereas deacon, priest, and bishop are *ordained* to the major orders. I use the word "tonsure" here because it is often used in this context and because it is appropriately descriptive: a bit of the hair is clipped as a symbol of self-abnegating ethos of any clerical order. However, sometimes the words "blessed" or "consecrated" are used interchangeably with "tonsure" (and sometimes "ordination" is used to describe the entrance into the minor orders, though this is incorrect and confusing—see the discussion of ordination in the next chapter). The distinction between minor and major orders is meaningful in Orthodox ecclesiology because of the conferral of greater authority, connection to the Eucharist, and role of the Holy Spirit that is part of ordination.

The precise duties or roles of the minor orders are generally known in practice, even if they are not richly substantiated or defined in the Orthodox Church's theology or ecclesiology. A reader reads the variable passages of scripture within a service (Epistles, Psalms, but not the Gospel) and might be called upon to lead a (non-Eucharistic) service in the absence of a priest. A cantor (chanter) chants and sings the hymns particular to any day or service. A subdeacon assists during the Eucharistic liturgy and cares for the altar and vestments. The subdiaconate is sometimes presented as a gateway into the major orders of clergy; in some traditions, a person will be tonsured a subdeacon before being ordained a deacon.

For all three of the minor orders, there is no canonical, theological, or pastoral prohibition on women's participation. There are certainly past examples of women serving in these roles and recent affirmations in present times, including the Rhodes Consultation report.[19]

But men still occupy the vast majority of these roles. Teva Regule suggests that "clericalization" of these roles is one possible reason for the exclusion of women from the minor orders.[20] In the past, in the case of a reader, someone—often a young person—was "set aside to study the Scriptures as well as all the liturgical books for the services and was to lead reader services if no priest was present,"[21] as well as to read the Epistle readings when the priest was present. Although there is no theological, liturgical, or traditional ladder from reader to priesthood (or from any other minor order to the priesthood), the order of reader has, in recent memory, become understood as the "first degree of Priesthood."[22] It is unclear why. Regule posits an influence from Roman Catholicism, in which "(at least prior to Vatican II) one needed to rise through the degrees of 'priesthood,' meaning the minor orders, in order to be ordained a presbyter."[23] This unwarranted connection with the priesthood may therefore have unnecessarily excluded women from serving in the minor orders of the Orthodox Church. The "stepping-stone" perception also discourages a richer appreciation of the vocation of each order.

When Orthodox Christians do not see women participating in the liturgy in the minor orders—which are theoretically open to women, the message is clear: women are less than men, not important, and unworthy of liturgical roles. This diminishment of women is damaging to everyone and prevents the Orthodox Church from benefitting from women's incarnational realities in the liturgy.

Sometimes in the United States and elsewhere women *function* within these roles—such as performing the duties of a reader—but

19. Conclusions of the Inter-Orthodox Consultation, "Place of Women," 32.

20. Regule, "Liturgy as Relationship," 8.

21. Regule, "Liturgy as Relationship," 8.

22. Hapgood, *Service Book*, 308.

23. Regule, "Liturgy as Relationship," 8.

are not tonsured/blessed to do this work by their priest or bishop. Within my lifetime there has been a visible increase in women serving as readers and cantors, but nearly all of them are not formally blessed or tonsured. Yet public and express acknowledgment of women's ministerial leadership is critical. One real-life example: an Orthodox friend of mine described a situation that "radicalized" her. In her parish, a middle-aged, clear-voiced woman had functioned as a reader for decades and knew the cycles of services and the liturgy better than the priest himself. Yet, this woman was passed over for the official, tonsured status of reader. Instead, during the bishop's visit to the parish, a young man who rarely came to services was publicly tonsured to much fanfare. My friend said that everyone accepted the tonsure of the man and the ignoring of the women's efforts without question and the next week she was back serving (unacknowledged and untonsured) as reader and the young man went back to rarely attending services.

This story illustrates an important point: without church-sanctioned roles and ministries for women in the minor orders, a woman's participation in these roles is unappreciated and unacknowledged. Women's participation is also never secure. I know other women who have essentially served in the capacity of reader or chanter, but then have been summarily supplanted when an officially tonsured man comes to their parish. When women are not tonsured into the roles they are already doing, then they are always subject to the caprice of those (men) in authority. This is minimized if a woman is officially acknowledged as a reader. If women are already carrying out these roles, they ought to be publicly tonsured to participate in the life of the Orthodox Church as members of the minor orders and participants in other aspects of leadership and governance.

## Ministry of Girls

In addition to women moving into all these areas of leadership and governance, the Orthodox Church ought to consider the ministry of girls. While the Orthodox Church has scant ancient precedent for children of either sex serving at the altar—instead, adult men were typically tonsured for this role—in many parishes in the United States today boys are welcomed as "altar servers." They help the priest conduct the liturgy, hold candles during the procession of the Eucharist through the church in the Great Entrance, and so on. Boys serving like this is presumably an influence from other Christian contexts. If the Orthodox Church is going to continue to develop these innovative roles for children during the liturgy, then girls ought to be included.

Girls are sometimes involved in the Holy Friday procession when they scatter flower petals as "little myrrh-bearers." Memorably, at one parish I've attended, two teenage girls held the shroud of Christ aloft and all parishioners who had just processed ducked underneath it on their way back into church. These are lovely customs and should continue. But when girls' involvement in the liturgy is so rare as to come around only once a year, the idea that this sort of liturgical participation is not normal for girls is underscored.

There is no reason for a prohibition of girls serving at the altar alongside boys. Sometimes one will hear the justification that menstruation prohibits girls from this service (see chapter 2 for a debunking of claims around menstruation and the Orthodox Church) or that only boys can be altar servers because only men can be priests. This is a post-facto justification of prohibiting girl altar servers at best. The experience of the Orthodox community seeing only boys and not girls offered the honor of altar service and liturgical experience only perpetuates misbegotten perception of girls (and therefore women) as unworthy and unfit for ministerial leadership in the local church and as second-class citizens in the church at large.[24]

24. An important issue for consideration with altar girls is the general impropriety and inadvisability of male clergy being alone with women or girls, given that the pre-liturgical preparations often involve just the priest and altar servers. If there were women in liturgical roles—readers, chanters, deaconesses—this would obviate these concerns. Additionally, there is the question of whether *any* minor—male or female—ought to be alone with clergy, although it is common for boy altar servers to arrive early to help prepare the vestry and sacristy for the service.

# LEADERSHIP: THE CHURCH OF OUR GRANDDAUGHTERS

The inclusion of women in roles of leadership, governance, and ministry will be readily accomplished by a church that has the interest and appreciation for women's skills, experiences, contributions, and incarnational realities. It is my hope that the Orthodox church of our granddaughters will be amply populated by women leaders in the parish and jurisdictional level, with women present at all conciliar efforts of the local or global Orthodox Church, and with women as readers, cantors, and subdeaconesses, and girls as altar servers (if the Orthodox Church continues to include children at the altar). New or restored tonsured roles ought to also be considered for women, such as "catechist" for those who teach children or adults and perhaps even "homilist" for women who have a talent for preaching.

Jesus Christ himself noted, "No one lights a lamp and puts it under a basket, but on a lampstand, and it gives light to all who are in the house" (Matt 5:15). Orthodox women's gifts and talents are often the metaphorical "lamp under the basket" in the Orthodox Church. May the Orthodox Church be inspired to place those gifts on the lampstand, may it "give light to all who are in the house" by inspiring the involvement of women in the governance and leadership of the Orthodox Church.

# 6

# Ordination

*I envision women as ordained deaconesses in the Orthodox*
*Church of our granddaughters; deaconesses who serve women,*
*men, and the mission of the church. I also envision the church*
*as capable of considering the possibility of other ordained*
*ministries for women.*

I once asked +Bishop Athanasios Akunda of Kisumu and all Western Kenya of blessed memory about the roles and responsibilities
of the then-newly consecrated deaconesses in Africa. His Beatitude
Theodoros II, Pope and Patriarch of Alexandria and All Africa,
had recently consecrated five women as deaconesses in 2017 in the
Democratic Republic of Congo, but their function in the church
was not clear to observers in the United States.

Bishop Akunda told me the deaconesses would likely continue
doing the same things that women were already doing in Africa—
in the Democratic Republic of Congo, in his area of Kenya, and
elsewhere—such as helping with the baptism of women and girls,
teaching catechesis, leading services in places where priests were
unavailable, and reading the Gospel in church. He tossed off this
list simply, as though these were the usual women's duties anywhere
in the Orthodox Christian world, but I was astounded. I have *never
heard a woman read the Gospel* in an Orthodox service. I told Bishop Akunda this, and he laughed in his affable way and said I should

visit Africa so that I could hear the proclamation of the Good News in a woman's voice.

Tragically, Bishop Akunda died an untimely death. I may or may not make it to Africa, but it's my fervent hope that our grand-daughters will hear women read the Gospel during Liturgy. I hope that my granddaughters will experience this in the form of the rein-stituted order of the ordained deaconess in the Orthodox Church. As of today, women are not part of any of the ordained major orders of clergy in the Orthodox Church, even though ordained deacon-esses, in different places and with different roles, were present in the first millennium, and, as just noted, they have been recently consecrated to do this work again in Africa.

Reinstituting the ordained order of deaconesses in the Ortho-dox Church is necessary to the vitality of the church of our grand-daughters. The Orthodox Church needs its women's incarnational realities in ordained ministry in order to fully live out its mission. With ample historical precedent and demonstrated current need, there is every reason for the Orthodox Church to move quickly to ordain deaconesses once again.

## ORDINATION: PAST

Many sources from the first thousand years of Christian history val-idate and illuminate the order of deaconess in the church, and this is important for a tradition like Orthodox Christianity that places a great deal of value on precedent. Here I will briefly summarize the presence of the deaconess in the ancient world, a presence that has been amply and much more thoroughly documented by other scholars.[1]

Saint Paul tells in his Letter to the Romans of a deaconess, Phoebe, whom we celebrate as a saint in the Orthodox Church, "I commend to you our sister Phoebe, a deacon of the church at Cenchreae, so that you may welcome her in the Lord as is fitting

---

1. For more thorough histories of the order of deaconesses, see Fitzgerald, *Women Deacons*; Karras, "Female Deacons"; Madigan and Osiek, *Ordained Women*; Theodorou, *'H Cheirotonia 'H Cheirothesia*; Vagaggaini, *Ordination of Women*; Wijngaards, *Ordained Women Deacons*; and Zagano, *Holy Saturday*.

for the saints, and help her in whatever she may require from you, for she has been a benefactor of many and of myself as well" (Rom 16:1–2). Though the orders of the clergy were not fully formed in the first century, the Orthodox Church understands Phoebe to be a proto member of what later developed into the ministry of the diaconate. Her appearance in icons shows us that she is a deaconess: she is typically holding an incense censer, indicative of the activity of members of the diaconate during services. Note the language for Phoebe in Romans is "deacon." Both "deacon" and "deaconess" were used interchangeably in the ancient church to refer to female members of the diaconate.[2] I typically use "deaconess" in my own writing because I find it a more elegant term that quickly distinguishes between women and men in the diaconate.[3]

Inscriptions from the ancient world validate the understanding of Phoebe as a deaconess and provide further evidence of the presence of deaconesses in the early church. For example, a tombstone reads: "Here lives the slave and bride of Christ, Sophia, the deacon, the second Phoebe."[4] And another: "Here lies the deacon Maria of pious and blessed memory, who according to the words of the apostle, raised children, sheltered guests, washed the feet of the saints, and shared her bread with the needy. Remember her, O Lord, when she comes into your kingdom."[5] In liturgical rubrics and architectural descriptions, the physical presence of deaconesses in the church and their participation in its liturgical life including processions is attested.[6]

Deaconesses are referenced in several canons of the church, which provide further witness to the presence of deaconesses in the

2. Fitzgerald, *Women Deacons*, xiv; see also footnote 1, xix.

3. Wives of deacons in the Orthodox Church sometimes use the title "deaconess" or "diakonissa." For a discussion of the word "deacon," its history, its application to women, and its translation, see Dzubinski and Stasson, *Women in the Mission*, 47–50.

4. Eisen, *Women Officeholders*, 159.

5. Eisen, *Women Officeholders*, 165.

6. For discussions of the physical space occupied by deaconesses in the early church, see Karras, "Female Deacons," 285–87; Moran, "Narthex of Deaconesses in Hagia Sophia"; and Taft, "Women at Church," 27–87, 62.

ancient world.[7] These canons address consequences if a deaconess betrays the confidence of the church and requirements, such as age and marital status. For example, a canon from the fifth-century Council of Chalcedon (451) stated, "A woman shall not receive the laying on of hands as a deaconess under forty years of age, and then only after searching examination."[8] Deaconesses were generally expected to be unmarried (or widowed), although, as is often the case in the canonical or historical record, there are exceptions.

The ordination rite for deaconesses is included in the earliest extant *Book of Needs* of the church, the Barberini Codex Gr. 336 from the eighth century, further illuminating deaconesses. This service book was composed in southern Italy based on a Constantinopolitan model. Deaconesses were ordained much like their male counterparts: by the bishop, at the altar, during Liturgy, and they received communion with the rest of the clergy. These words are included:

> Lord, Lord, who do not reject women offering themselves and wishing to minister in your holy houses in accordance with what is fitting, but receive them in an order of ministers; bestow the grace of your Holy Spirit also on this your servant who wishes to offer herself to you, and fill her with the grace of the diaconate, as you gave the grace of your diaconate to Phoebe whom you called to the work of ministry.[9]

The roles of deaconesses appear to have been diverse and our current understanding of them comes from a variety of sources, including inscriptions, canon law, and conciliar and other church documents.[10] In the gender-divided ancient world women in

7. Detractors point to canons that appear to ban or dismiss the idea of ordained deaconesses (such as those from Nîmes in 396; Orange in 441; Epaone in 517; or Orleans in 533), but these canons come from *local* and *western* councils and are not part of the dogmatic and canonical tradition of the Orthodox Church, as asserted at the Quinisext Council in 692.

8. "Canons of Council of Chalcedon," Canon 15.

9. Bradshaw, *Ordination Rites*, 138.

10. Such as Didascalia Apostolorum (third century), Apostolic Constitutions (fourth century), canon 40 of the Council of Trullo (seventh century),

particular led private lives and only appeared in public in circumscribed situations. Therefore, deacons typically ministered to men and deaconesses ministered to women.[11] Deaconesses visited women in their homes, took the Eucharist to those women were ill, helped with adult female baptism and catechesis, and escorted women when visiting a priest. But other roles fulfilled by deaconesses don't seem to have been gender-determined, such as participating in processions and serving as agents of the bishop in tasks of hospitality and philanthropy.[12]

The ordained order of deaconesses was never banned or officially discontinued. And yet, deaconesses became scarce around the twelfth century.[13] There are likely several contributing factors for this decline, including the monastic influence on parish liturgical life, which saw monastic ways of worship replacing "cathedral" rites (meaning, parish settings). Liturgical conventions from a male monastic context left no space, literally, for the participation of deaconesses. Other factors may have been the decrease in adult converts, which meant deaconesses were not in demand for their role in women's baptisms and catechesis (though, as noted above, these were certainly not the only roles of deaconesses), geopolitical pressure on the Byzantine empire (as the Ottomans invaded, their sensibilities around women, which did not allow for engagement in worship and leadership, may have influenced the Orthodox Church), and the putative connection between women's bodies and impurity, discussed in chapters 2 and 3 (which included a "logic" that if women were impure they did not belong near the altar).[14]

Notably, the decline of ordained deaconesses was a part of a larger decline of the diaconate as whole. Although men are still ordained deacons today, the fullness of this order has never been recovered. Today deacons are often considered to be little more

---

and the canons of two ecumenical councils: First Council of Nicea, canon 19 and Council of Chalcedon, canon 15 (fourth and fifth centuries).

11. Karras, "Female Deacons in the Byzantine Church," 272–316.

12. Karras, "Female Deacons in the Byzantine Church," 277–87.

13. For a discussion of the fading presence of deaconesses, see Karras, "Female Deacons," 277.

14. See Blastares, "Concerning Women Deacons and Widows," 110–12.

than either liturgical helpers or those on a "stepping-stone" toward the priesthood, rather than members of an important order in its own right, with a unique ministry. (Note the minor orders, though much less developed in the first place—are also being reduced in this way; see previous chapter.)

Opponents of the reinstitution of deaconesses posit their own reasons for the decline of the order. Some have recently suggested the Orthodox Church stopped ordaining women because it "came to its senses" and recognized women should never be in authority over men.[15] This claim does not make sense within Orthodox ecclesiology. Here is a critical point about the diaconate and authority: while all ordained orders bear the *authority* of the church by their very nature, the work of the diaconate is *service*, and the characterization of the diaconate wherein one group exercises authority over another misconstrues and subverts this truth.

Oriental Orthodox brothers and sisters of the Orthodox Church have recently reinstated deaconesses,[16] and the Roman Catholic Church continues to consider the possibility of deaconesses for the twentieth-first century. At the time of this writing, a commission appointed by Pope Francis is working on this issue. Most germane and important for such considerations in the Orthodox Church is the reinstitution of deaconesses recently in Africa. The Synod of Alexandria understood the documents of the 2016 Holy and Great Council as affirming the ability of local Orthodox Churches to minister to local needs, including recognizing deaconesses. It is widely known that the original intention of the Patriarch of Alexandria was to ordain these women to the diaconate. However, donors outside of Africa threatened to cut off income streams to the African Church if the Patriarch went ahead with ordinations. The African Church is not self-sufficient; it is dependent on outside funding. As a concession, the Patriarch "consecrated" these women as deaconesses in 2017, rather than ordaining them. The perceived distinction between a "blessing" or "consecration" and an "ordination" in the Orthodox Church is important, as discussed in

15. See Mitchell, *Disappearing Deaconess*.
16. See Armenian Orthodox Church, "Historic Ordination."

the previous chapter. Interestingly, the deaconesses in Africa were consecrated deaconesses in a ritual that appears to occupy a space in between a tonsure to the minor orders and ordination to the major orders.[17]

The Patriarch went on to consecrate several other women in Sierra Leone and elsewhere in Africa before obliquely stating that the Church of Alexandria would not continue in this experiment, that it was "suspended for the time being," presumably because of ongoing financial pressure.[18] Today, African theologians and clergy continue to publicly support the prospect of a continued reinstitution of deaconesses in the Alexandrian Patriarchate. Fr. Njorge John Ngige maintains that there is "no canonical or doctrinal opposition to deaconesses" and that deaconesses may be rightfully welcome in the church today for apostolic and missionary reasons:

> The church is apostolic, the church is for all people, when men and women receive the same grace, receive the Eucharist, they are a part of the mission of the church. . . . The church does not discriminate based on color, race, nationality, thus women are fully included in the mission of the church including deaconesses.[19]

The rest of the Orthodox Church can learn two valuable lessons from the deaconesses in Africa. One, that money is—unfortunately and sadly—a concern when moving forward with women in the diaconate. Rather than the central concern being building up the body of Christ, sometimes it is the tearing down of initiatives by the wealthy. Second, despite the financial pressures and suspension of the deaconess project in Africa, these twenty-first-century deaconesses offer a precedent (even if imperfect and cautionary) for the reinstitution of this order.[20]

17. See my discussion of this in two articles: "Women Deacons in Africa," and "Women Willing to Offer."

18. Vasiliadis, "Final Report."

19. Ngige, "IOTA Missiology Seminar."

20. For a longer discussion of the realities of the deaconesses of Africa and reactions to them outside of Africa, see my "Status of the Reinstitution of Deaconesses."

# ORDINATION: TODAY

The reinstitution of the order of ordained deaconesses has been under consideration by bishops, theologians, and laity for some time across the Orthodox world—from late nineteenth- and early twentieth-century Russia,[21] to 1980s Greece, to contemporary Africa.[22] In the words of eminent theologian Metropolitan Kallistos Ware:

> We should try to go ahead with the revival of the order of deaconess. That has been discussed for many years. Some people were already discussing it at the beginning of [the twentieth] century in the Orthodox world. Nothing has yet been done. The order of deaconess was never abolished, it merely fell into disuse. Should we not revive it?[23]

There are many reasons for the reinstitution of deaconesses today. One is the strong historical precedent, acknowledging that the reinstitution of the order would involve discernment and creativity in configuring it for today's needs. The second reason we ought to ordain is that many within the Orthodox Church urge us to do so. This was the case with the Rhodes Consultation thirty-five years ago, which was convened by the Ecumenical Patriarch:

> The apostolic order of deaconesses should be revived. . . . Such a revival would represent a positive response to many of the needs and demands of the contemporary world in many spheres. . . . The revival of women deacons in the Orthodox Church would emphasize in a special way the dignity of woman and give recognition to her contribution to the work of the Church as a whole.[24]

21. For a review of the consideration of deaconesses in the pre-Soviet Russian Church, see Beliakova, "Women in the Church," 47–62. Interestingly, in this context, the restoration of deaconesses was promoted as a wise move on the part of the Russian Church in reaction to secularization.

22. For a list and description of contemporary calls, see "Calls for the Rejuvenation," *Saint Phoebe Center for the Deaconess.*

23. Regule, "Interview with Metropolitan Kallistos."

24. Conclusions of the Inter-Orthodox Consultation, "The Place of the Woman," 17–18.

We also hear the call to reinstate deaconesses echoed twice in the recent document commissioned and approved by the Ecumenical Patriarch, *For the Life of the World: Toward a Social Ethos of the Orthodox Church*. One example comes after a discussion of the innate equality of men and women and the Orthodox Church's failure to consistently live up to this teaching, the document turns to roles of women in the Orthodox Church today, including the diaconate:

> The Church must also remain attentive to the promptings of the Spirit in regard to the ministry of women, especially in our time, when many of the most crucial offices of ecclesial life—theologians, seminary professors, canonists, readers, choir directors, and experts in any number of professions that benefit the community of faith—are occupied by women in increasingly great numbers; and the Church must continue to consider how women can best participate in building up the body of Christ, including a renewal of the order of the female diaconate for today.[25]

The second reference to deaconesses comes at the very end of the document, as part of a hopeful vision of the Orthodox Church moving into the future.[26]

In addition to the historical precedent and recent calls, there is real *need* for deaconesses today in the Orthodox Church. The Orthodox Church needs the transformative outpouring of women's gifts into its life and into the world that would result from the reinstitution of the order. Women are needed to serve as deaconesses by virtue of their baptism, on the basis of the unique gifts each human person has to offer. The Orthodox Church also needs women's gifts because women have a different incarnational reality than men, which means they have different gifts to offer *as women*. Women or men can offer the expertise of diaconal ministries as chaplains, administrators, pastoral counselors, but only women can offer the gifts garnered from their incarnational realities and experiences as women.

25. Ecumenical Patriarch, *For the Life of the World*, ch. 29. As acknowledged in previous chapters, I was on the special commission that composed this document.

26. Ecumenical Patriarch, *For the Life of the World*, ch. 82.

*Women* need women's gifts; they need woman-to-woman ministry. This is not an antiquated idea that we in enlightened America or Europe have outgrown. There is a reason I belong to an all-woman book group, and there is wisdom behind the decision of the hospice where I volunteered to pair female respite caregivers with female patients. There are times when a woman needs to be ministered to by another woman, several of which have been addressed in the book (postpartum prayers and miscarriage) and many that have not (for example: marriage, divorce, abuse, issues relating to the female body). This sort of ministry happens informally in parishes (and book groups), but the good that could be done would be greatly magnified if there were theologically and pastorally trained women ordained as deaconesses, ready to minister to other women, with the oversight, support, and authority of the Orthodox Church.

The *whole* church—not only women—needs women's gifts. Because of their different incarnational realities, women have, for example, a different perspective on authority, its judicious use, its squandering, its misuse, its abuse, from which the whole church would benefit. Women have a different lived experience of—and have learned different lessons from—sexual abuse and assault, from which the whole church would benefit. Women have a different view of child-rearing, marriage, and family life, from which the whole church would benefit—and so on. Women have an understanding of giving and sustaining life from which the whole church and the planet would benefit.

Some of these gifts are already being shared with the Orthodox Church in the twenty-first century—women now serve on parish councils, teach in seminaries, and so on, as reported in chapter 5. This is wonderful, but it does not reflect the ways in which women's gifts would be truly infused into the life of the Orthodox Church if women were ordained to the diaconate, and thus had the sacramental blessing of this ministry, enlivening their gifts by the grace of the Holy Spirit and connecting them to the sacramental life of the church. The recognition of both the need for woman-to-woman ministry and the ways in which women's gifts benefit the entire church were among the motivations for the Patriarchate of Alexandria to begin to reinstitute the order of deaconesses in Africa.

The entire church would benefit from women entering the diaconate because of the fresh possibilities of men and women working together in ordained ministry. There will undoubtably be a sacramental synergy when, for example, a deaconess and a priest go together to minister to a married couple grieving a miscarriage. There are very rich and very real possibilities for men and women to cooperate within ordained ministry, thus serving the church and the world.

A further benefit of the reinstitution of deaconesses is that it would inevitably prompt a revival of the entire diaconate through the attention and merit it would bring to the order, and this would be a most welcome development. Ordained deaconesses would be part of a reinvigorated and healthy diaconate as a whole, which would foster a revival of the diaconal mission of the Orthodox Church. The diaconal mission of the church, the *service ethos* of the Church, is, in fact, the authentic church and the fullest expression of the kingdom here on earth.

Women should be *ordained* to the diaconate, not only tonsured (or consecrated or blessed) into minor orders, because ordination offers—as we understand it in the Orthodox Church—the oversight, support, and authority of the church, and ordination connects the deaconess with the sacramental life of the church. The oversight and support of the church are linked; they both require deep relationships and mutual accountability between the ordained and the bishop, the ordained and the parish, and with the ordained and her peers.

Authority is important because the authority of the Orthodox Church is bestowed upon the person being ordained, and this is experienced and sealed in the epiclesis, the invocation of the Holy Spirit, which is an aspect of ordination that is unique to the major orders. We understand the invocation of the Holy Spirit as central to the sacraments of the church. A sample of the language in the ordination of the deaconess: "send down upon her the abundant gifts of your Holy Spirit," and in another rite the prayer asks God to "bestow the grace of your Holy Spirit"[27] on the deaconess. The authority of the church is bestowed in ordination, and it is sustained through the service, the *diakonia*, of the ordained person. And there are pragmatic consequences of authority that come with ordination, consequences that are not about coercive power, but are about *possibility*. When authority is conferred, it changes the relationship between that person and the surrounding community, and this has consequences.

Ordination connects the ordained and his or her ministry to the sacramental life of the church. Every sacrament depends on the sacrament of sacraments, the Eucharist. The centrality of the Eucharist in the ordination rites for deaconesses is clear. According to two manuscript traditions, the deaconess was "ordained during the Eucharist, at exactly the same point during the liturgy as for the male deacon."[28] A few minutes later, the "newly ordained female deacon received Communion at the hand of the Archbishop, who then gave her the chalice, which she received and placed back on the altar."[29] The ordination of the deaconess is bound up with the Eucharist. The connection with the sacrament of sacraments deepened when the deaconesses took communion to women who were ill or homebound. This practice was attested to as early as the third century, and there are also textual references to deaconesses taking communion to women in prison. In bearing the Eucharist to women in such situations, the deaconess become a means for the extension and expression of the sacramental life of the church.

Ordination, as a sacrament of the Orthodox Church, is transformative in the sense that it changes a person through the direct presence and visitation of the Holy Spirit and changes that person's relationship with her community through the authority and confidence conferred on her by the church. This transformation—as with all the sacraments—requires that the ordained live a life of

27. Quoted in Fitzgerald, *Women Deacons*, 85.

28. Karras, "Female Deacons," 300. The deaconess's ordination took place immediately following the end of the anaphora, after the royal doors were reopened. (The anaphora is the thanksgiving prayer that offers bread and wine to be consecrated as the body and blood of Christ.)

29. Karras, "Female Deacons," 301. This takes place after she is vested with the diaconal orarion.

the Spirit and bring the Spirit's work to fruition through her own action. Ordination involves a unique incorporation into the structure and life of the church and reflects a lifelong transformation and commitment, unlike lay ministries which can be temporary. These are the particular blessings conferred in ordination of which women are worthy as deaconesses.

We should ordain deaconesses in the Orthodox Church because the sacramental blessing of this ministry will allow women's gifts to be truly infused into the life of the Orthodox Church, which will be to the glory of God and the benefit of all. The gifts of women will be more fully given to the church and the world; these gifts will be honored, celebrated, and realized in new, wonderful, and unanticipated ways; and that the presence of deaconesses will prompt an effloresce of service, healing, well-being, flourishing, and hope in the life of the Orthodox Church today.

## ORDINATION: CHURCH OF OUR GRANDDAUGHTERS

Ordination in the Orthodox Church follows a canonical pattern with respect to the three major orders: one must be ordained a deacon before being ordained a priest and ordained a priest before being ordained a bishop. Although this sequence is not inevitable; many deacons remain as "permanent" deacons. Detractors or simply skeptics of deaconesses often inquire, "Won't ordaining deaconesses inevitably bring about female priests?" Or, "What is the connection between deaconesses and the priesthood?"[30] Often—but not always—these questions have the phrase "slippery slope" attached to them and a cast of anxiety around women and the priesthood that makes the questioner resistant to deaconesses.

The Orthodox Church has ample historical precedent for deaconesses, but none for female priests, and this alone puts us on very

30. For discussions of women and the priesthood in the Orthodox Church, see Wilson, "Elizabeth Behr-Sigel's Trinitarian Case," and Ladouceur, "Ordination of Women to the Priesthood." Ladouceur's chapter is helpful in its overview of the arguments against women as priests in the Orthodox Church and in his proposed shift to a pastoral perspective.

different tracks of conversation about either possibility within the Orthodox Church today. In our ecclesiology, each of the major orders—deacon, priest, bishop—has its own, distinct expression; the diaconate is not merely a way point to the priesthood, and, therefore, we cannot draw foregone conclusions about any progression from deaconess to priest. All this being said, it is absolutely true that while ordaining deaconesses today will not inevitably lead to female priests, it *will* inevitably lead to *conversation* about women in the priesthood.

The Orthodox community has no need to be afraid of this conversation, which has barely even begun. Our ecclesiology of the ordained orders, our robust theological anthropology, and our reticence to change means that the Orthodox Church will never hastily ordain women to the priesthood. If women are priests in the Orthodox Church at some point in the future, it will be because it arrived at this conclusion through a thoughtful process and with the guidance of the Holy Spirit. We ought to welcome this conversation about women in the priesthood (and the episcopate).[31]

Another comment heard from detractors or skeptics is the concern that the Orthodox Church will schism or divide if women are ordained to any major order. I cannot overemphasize two responses. One, the Orthodox Church is *already in schism over women and their roles in the church*. We are bleeding away younger generations (and some older ones, too) because it is both incomprehensible and entirely unacceptable to these people to stay in a church community that only honors the gifts of men and not women in ministry. As a friend recently commented in reaction to the question of why deaconesses are needed today, "The Orthodox Church is not fine as it is." Two, *fear of schism or division ought not be a yardstick for considering change in the Orthodox Church*. If the Orthodox Church changes its practices regarding women out of fidelity to its understanding of the truth, any possibility of division should not be a concern.

Given the precedent, clear need, and promise for the mission of the church, the Orthodox Church has every reason to ordain deaconesses in time for the church of our granddaughters. Support

31. See my "Flourishing Diaconate," 151–65.

for ordination of deaconesses will ideally come from synods of bishops, not just a lone bishop.

Reinstitution of the ordained order of deaconess would involve a creative re-imagination of how the order would best serve the Orthodox Church today. While the historical sources will be important in informing this re-imagination, they will not be determinative; deaconesses for the twenty-first century will be different from deaconesses in the ancient church, though in continuity with them. Deaconesses in Africa might have different roles and responsibilities than deaconesses in America, or Romania.

I envision women who lead lives of service and are theologically and pastorally trained ministering as deaconesses in our granddaughters' church. I imagine this coming about through the collective work of the laity and the hierarchy, with a synod of bishops with the input of the laity, especially women approving guidelines for deaconesses and ordaining them.[32] I see these deaconesses of the twenty-first century as engaged in various types of service, including philanthropy, administration, chaplaincy, social work, catechesis, and pastoral care to women and men of the parish. I see them serving at the altar during the Liturgy and other services.[33] I see the Orthodox Church of our granddaughters as abundantly capable of the conversation about women in the priesthood or the episcopate. I envision a future in which our granddaughters don't only hear about women reading the Gospel in faraway lands but hear the good news directly from the mouths of deaconesses in their own parishes and perhaps read the Gospel themselves.

32. One such set of parameters for the reinstitution of this order appears in Saint Catherine's Vision, "A Call for the Rejuvenation of the Ministry of the Ordained Deaconess."

33. Anecdotally, I know of several people in the Orthodox Church who are amenable to the possibility of deaconesses but draw the line at liturgical service both because of perceived lack of precedent and because of concerns about "optics." For me, the development of liturgical service for the deaconess is critical as an expression of full participation in the life of the church in its tangible witness to the sacramental service of deaconesses.

# Conclusion

*I hope this book is obsolete by the time of the church of our granddaughters. A book about the diminishment, denigration, and disenfranchisement of women in the Orthodox Church will no longer be needed because the Orthodox Church will be putting its ideals into practice. Our granddaughters will be valued for their personhood and their incarnational realities as women, and the whole church will benefit and better live out its mission as a result.*

The changes I advocate for in this book will affirm and enliven the authentic, diaconal mission of the Orthodox Church. The integration of women and their incarnational realities will better allow the church to live out its service mission. The church will be true to itself and authentically offer the Eucharist, as we pray in the Divine Liturgy, "on behalf of all and for all." This is critical for the health and continuation of the Orthodox Church. May this be so for the church of our granddaughters.

As I wrote in the introduction, this book comes from a place of deep love for the Orthodox Church that started in my hometown parish and has grown through my years as an Orthodox practitioner and scholar observing, studying, considering, and praying about women in the Orthodox Church. When women are ill-treated and ignored, this causes the whole body of Christ to suffer, as abundantly demonstrated within these pages and witnessed in my own life. Simultaneously, the Orthodox Church teaches that this should not be so. *Will the Orthodox Church align its present-day practices with its fundamental teachings?* It is my fervent hope and prayer that such changes will be made in time for the church of our granddaughters.

But this hope is clouded by several worries. There is a larger tendency within the Orthodox Church today to resist all change—whether healthy or unhealthy—only for the sake of creating a bulwark against the fragmentation of culture around us. I am sympathetic; I am unnerved by the swift and dehumanizing changes that affect every quarter of contemporary life, much of which is actively hostile to the church's incarnational anthropology. Walking into a church and singing the same hymns I sang as a child and that my father and his parents, on back through the generations, sang makes me grateful for the Orthodox Church as a sanctuary of continuity and steadfastness. It is reassuring to know that the Orthodox Church has no record of rash response to pressures from the world, that safeguards are organically in place that prevent hasty change of any sort, and Orthodoxy has a very different and sturdy ecclesiology that lacks the same weaknesses or fracture points as other communities. But these are not reasons for stagnation. Just as change is not good for its own sake, stasis is not good for its own sake.

The Orthodox Church ought not alter its ways just because of changes in the wider culture or a perceived need to adapt to the times, but the wider culture may on occasion justifiably prompt the Orthodox Church to revisit its own priorities and practices. It may even serve to hold it accountable for its own teachings. There is no doubt that the advancement of women into all manner of professions and skills in the modern era combined with the examples of other Christian communities ordaining women as major clergy have raised questions about roles of women in Orthodoxy. Some cite secular cultural change as a reason for not altering the Orthodox Church's practices regarding women, promoting a sort of reactionary digging in and holding to the status quo. But this is neither the logical nor the inevitable conclusion; as I have shown in the book, a fuller inclusion of women in the life of the church would be a fulfillment of our history and theology, not a departure. In pre-Soviet Russia, for example, concerns about secularization and non-Orthodox influence were reasons to *support* the reinstitution of deaconesses. It was deemed desirable for women to offer their skills and talents in the context of the church, rather than exclusively in their secular professions or in other charitable institutions.[1] The pre-Soviet Russian Church was able to open the possibility of adjusting rituals and roles for the benefit of the church, including the reinstitution of deaconesses, alongside of women's expanded roles in society. This can be an example to us today.

Another concern about the Orthodox Church today is its state of discourse and power. Vocal minorities (sometimes comprised of clergy) are often vicious and loud and, more worrisome, these voices are sometime given credence. Individuals will always say nasty and incorrect things, but the greater problem is that such tone and content is sometimes affirmed and accepted within the Orthodox Church. There is also a worrisome connection between this discourse and power and money. The quintessential example of male power and money determining outcomes was cited in chapter 6: the Patriarch of Alexandria intended to ordain women in Africa but downgraded to a consecration due to influential donors outside of Africa threatening to interfere with funding sources if an ordination took place, and the Patriarch later suspended the project.

Women are degraded and discriminated against within the Orthodox Church through money, power, and the tolerance of derogatory and demeaning discourse. A natural consequence of this potent combination is a culture of fear—fear of change; fear of doing the right thing because of the consequences and possible "division." Those who cite the possibility of division as reason for not changing the Orthodox Church's practices around women are blind, perhaps willfully so, to the ways that women's realities in the Orthodox Church are *already divisive*, driving women (and men) away from the Orthodox Church in droves in a silent schism. Furthermore, correcting the Orthodox Church's practices regarding women will bring a better alignment with its teachings, moving it closer to the kingdom. Any "division" that results from the Orthodox Church becoming truer to its mission should not be a concern.

1. See Beliakova, "Women in the Church," 47–62.

Change of the kind I propose in this book is not capitulation, instead it is a courageous response to the real needs of the Orthodox Church that will promote flourishing and fulfillment of its mission. It is time for the Orthodox Church to thoughtfully change its practices around women, not in a reactive manner but a proactive manner.

Many steps can be immediately taken to align the Orthodox Church's practices with its theology at the parish, council, or synod level. Across the autocephalous churches and within jurisdictions these changes may look different in order to minister to local needs. Uniformity is not required, but there ought to be unity between practice and theology. Parishes within an Orthodox Church (or jurisdiction) that have affirmed women and girls' approaching the chalice regardless of their menstrual cycle can immediately begin discussion around this matter, educating the faithful from the pulpit, at coffee hour, and in small groups. More Orthodox Churches, through councils or synods, can either adopt the Churching and miscarriage prayers already blessed in other Orthodox Churches or can commission a group of women scholars to create new versions, including a Churching for adopted children and prayers specific to stillbirth and early infant death. Bishops can tonsure women as readers, chanters, and subdeaconesses, and women can be incorporated more thoroughly into Orthodox Church leadership, working in chancery offices, as iconographers, church lawyers, and so forth. Finally, a synod of bishops can move to reinstitute the ordained order of deaconess by convening a commission to design a plan of implementation that includes hierarchical, parish, and peer input and support. All these changes regarding women in the Orthodox Church—and variations on these themes—are easily within reach of the Orthodox Church because they are not a deviation from the truth, but an authentic expression of it.

*Church of Our Granddaughters* constitutes one vision of the minimum that is necessary for the Orthodox Church to rightly minister to its women, to provide a holistic and Christ-centered community for all its members, and to live up to its service mission. There will be more to do, and others will have different priorities and different visions of how to go about these changes. The

Orthodox Church needs many women's voices from many areas of expertise shaping its future. I welcome all perspectives—from women and men—on how to better the lives of women in the Orthodox Church; mine is by no means the only one.

A friend and I were in a conversation with a newly named bishop a few years ago. She surprised me with her directness when she said to him, "Be *bold* in your ministry as a bishop! Make real, meaningful changes. You have the best job security in the world; use it for good and don't make decisions out of fear, instead make them out of conviction for what's right." This is the crux: for thorough, authentic, and lasting change to come to the Orthodox Church regarding women, that change must ultimately be enacted *by men* because men hold the ultimate decision-making authority in every part of the Orthodox Church. Women can (and should) organize, publish scholarship, seek audiences with hierarchs, work with the laity, and so on, but it is the governing all-male hierarchy—bishops and synods of bishops—who must initiate these changes (ideally with ample consultation with women).

It is my hope and prayer that the male hierarchy of the Orthodox Church will be bold in its dedication to the doctrine of the Incarnation and its significance to all people and therefore swiftly correct practices and prayers around menstruation, Churching, and miscarriage. It is my hope and prayer that the male hierarchy will find the courage and conviction to bring women into leadership and governance positions, including tonsuring women to the minor orders and ordaining women to the diaconate. It is my hope and prayer that the entire Orthodox Church—clergy and laity—will work together to bring about these changes. All the changes to ritual and ministries that I discuss in this book are within easy reach of the entire Orthodox Church, should we "be bold."

In the Orthodox Church of our granddaughters, there will not be a strict uniformity of qualities and gifts offered by women, nor will women make the Orthodox Church perfect. Yet the whole church will benefit from bringing the Orthodox Church's practices concerning women into alignment with its life-giving theology. The whole church will benefit from infusing women into practice and ministry. A shift in practices and expansion of women's roles will bring women's incarnational realities into the church in a new and holistic way. A friend recently asked how the Orthodox Church will change when women are fully welcomed. My answer was that we cannot possibly know—this is something that we have never experienced.

But it is something that we *can* experience; something *quite possible* for the Orthodox Church. We have ample resources for the work ahead. Let us do it for the sake of the church of our granddaughters; indeed, for our granddaughters and our grandsons.

# Bibliography

Afentoulidou, Eirini. "The Childbed Prayers in the Byzantine Euchologia: Preliminary Notes." In "Byzantine Prayer Books as Sources for Social History and Daily Life," edited by Claudia Rapp et al. *Jahrbuch der Österreichischen Byzantinistik* 67 (2017) 173–211.

———. Review of *Maternal Body: A Theology of Incarnation from the Christian East*. *Journal of Orthodox Christian Studies* 3.1 (2020) 99–101.

Armenian Orthodox Church. "Historic Ordination: Tehran Prelacy of the Armenian Church Ordains Deaconesses." https://armenianweekly.com/2018/01/16/historic-ordination-tehran-diocese-armenian-church-ordains-deaconess/.

Arranz, Miguel. "Les Sacrements de l'ancien Euchologe constantinopolitain: deuxième partie: Admission dans l'Eglise des enfants des familles chrétiennes ('premier catéchumenat')." *Orientalia Christiana Periodica* 49 (1983) 284–302.

Assembly of Bishops. "Orthodox Churches in 21st Century America: A Parish Life Study, Executive Summary." https://www.assemblyofbishops.org/news/news-archive/2018/study-orthodox-christian-churches-21st-century.

———. "Perinatal and Infant Loss Draft: A Resource for Orthodox Christian Pastors." Unpublished paper.

Axia Women. https://www.axiawomen.org.

Basil of Caesarea. "On the Origin of Humanity, Discourse 1." In *On the Human Condition*, translated by Nonna Verna Harrison, 31–48. Crestwood, NY: St. Vladimir's Seminary Press, 2005.

Behr, John. "From Adam to Christ: From Male and Female to Being Human." *The Wheel* 13/14 (2018) 19–32.

Behr-Sigel, Elisabeth. *The Ministry of Women in the Church*. Translated by Fr. Steven Bingham. Crestwood, NY: St. Vladimir's Seminary Press, 1990.

Beliakova, Nadezhda. "Women in the Church: Conceptions of Orthodox Theologians in Twentieth Century." In *Orthodox Christianity and Gender: Dynamics of Tradition, Culture, and Lived Practice*, edited by Helena Kupari and Elena Voula, 47–62. London: Routledge, 2020.

Biale, Rachel. *Women and Jewish Law*. New York: Schocken, 1984.

Blastares, Matthew. *The Alphabetical Collection, Sexuality, Marriage, and Celibacy in Byzantine Law.* Translated by Patrick Demetrios Viscuso. Brookline, MA: Holy Cross Orthodox Press, 2008.

Bouteneff, Patricia Fann. "Invisible Leaders in the Orthodox Church." https://www.aphaiaresources.com/2016/09/05/invisible-leaders-in-the-orthodox-church/.

Bouteneff, Peter. *Beginnings: Ancient Christian Readings of the Biblical Creation Narratives.* Crestwood, NY: St. Vladimir's Seminary Press, 2008.

Bradshaw, Paul. *Ordination Rites of the Ancient Churches East and West.* Collegeville, MN: Liturgical, 1990.

Bragwynne, Sarah, and Sasha Rose Oxnard. *A Sacred Beginning: Nurturing Your Body, Mind, and Soul during Baby's First Forty Days.* Chesterton, IN: Ancient Faith, 2021.

Butcher, Brian. "Gender and Orthodox Theology: Vistas and Vantage Points." In *Orthodox Christianity and Gender,* edited by Helen Kupari and Elina Voula, 25–46. London: Routledge, 2020.

"Canons of the Council of Chalcedon 451," Canon 15. In *Nicene and Post-Nicene Fathers,* 2nd series, vol. 14, edited by Philip Schaff and Henry Wace, translated by Henry Percival. Buffalo, NY: Christian Literature, 1900. Revised and edited for New Advent by Kevin Knight. http://www.newadvent.org/fathers/3811.htm.

Clark, Elizabeth A. "Patrons, Not Priests: Women and Power in Late Ancient Christianity." *Gender and History* 2 (1990) 253–73.

Conclusions of the Inter-Orthodox Consultation. "The Place of the Woman in the Orthodox Church and the Question of the Ordination of Women." Rhodes, Greece: 30 October-November 1988. Minneapolis: Light and Life, 1990.

Deville, Adam A. J. *Everything Hidden Shall Be Revealed: Ridding the Church of Abuses of Sex and Power.* Brooklyn, NY: Angelico, 2019.

Didascalia Apostolorum. In *Early Christian Writings,* edited by Peter Kirby, translated by R. Hugh Connolly, 22. 1929. Reprint, Oxford: Clarendon, 2015. http://www.earlychristianwritings.com/text/didascalia.html.

Dionysius of Alexandria. *The Letters and Other Remains of Dionysius of Alexandria.* Edited by C. L. Feltoe. New York: Macmillian, 1904. https://www.gutenberg.org/files/36539/36539-h/36539-h.htm.

Dzubinski, Leanne M., and Anneke H. Stasson. *Women in the Mission of the Church: Their Opportunities and Obstacle throughout Christian History.* Grand Rapids: Baker Academic, 2021.

Ecumenical Patriarchate. *For the Life of the World: Toward a Social Ethos of the Orthodox Church.* Brookline, MA: Holy Cross Orthodox Press, 2020. https://www.goarch.org/social-ethos.

Eisen, Ute E. *Women Officeholders in Early Christianity: Epigraphical and Literary Studies.* Collegeville, MN: Liturgical, 2000.

Evdokimov, Paul. *Orthodoxy.* New York: New City, 2011.

————. *Women and the Salvation of the World*. Translated by Anthony Gythiel. Crestwood, NY: St. Vladimir's Seminary Press, 1994.

Farley, Lawrence R. "Menstruation and Communion of Women." In *Feminism and Tradition: Quiet Reflections on Ordination and Communion*, 161–77. Crestwood, NY: St. Vladimir's Seminary Press, 2012.

Fitzgerald, Kyriaki Karidoyanes. *Women Deacons in the Orthodox Church: Called to Holiness and Ministry*. Brookline, MA: Holy Cross Orthodox Press, 1999.

Frost, Carrie Frederick. "A Flourishing Diaconate Will Ground—Not Predetermine—Conversation about Women in the Priesthood." In *Women and Ordination of the Orthodox Church: Explorations in Theology and Practice*, edited by Gabrielle Thomas and Elena Narinskaya, 151–65. Eugene, OR: Cascade, 2020.

————. *Maternal Body: A Theology of Incarnation from the Christian East*. Mahweh, NJ: Paulist, 2019.

————. "Matters of Birth and Death in the Ecumenical Patriarchate and Russian Orthodox Church's Social Statements." *Studies in Christian Ethics, A Special Issue: A Fresh Vision for Orthodox Social Ethics* 35.2 (2021) 1–15.

————. "Pastoral Care of Perinatal and Infant Loss: The Importance of Rites." *Orthodox Christian Association of Medicine, Psychology, and Religion Newsletter*. November 2015.

————. "The Status of the Reinstitution of Deaconesses in the Orthodox Church Today: Consecrated in Africa, Considered Elsewhere." *Ecumenical Trends*, 51.3 (May/June 2022) 7–11.

————. "Women Deacons in Africa; Not in America." *Public Orthodoxy*. https://publicorthodoxy.org/2017/03/02/alexandria-deaconesses/.

————. "Women Willing to Offer Themselves: The Historic Consecration of Deaconesses in Africa." *The Wheel*, March 2, 2017. https://www.wheeljournal.com/blog/2017/3/2/carrie-frederick-frost-women-willing-to-offer-themselves-the-historic-consecration-of-deaconesses-in-africa.

Galadza, Peter. "The Priest's Wife: A Vocation in Her Own Right—and Rite." *Journal for the Study of Marriage and Spirituality* 21.1 (2015) 43–52.

Glibetić, Nina. "Orthodox Liturgical Rites at Pregnancy Loss: Ritual Responses to Miscarriage, Stillbirth, and Abortion in Late Byzantium." *Journal of Orthodox Christian Studies* 4.2 (2021) 151–79.

Greek Orthodox Archdiocese of America. "The Divine Liturgy of Saint Basil the Great." http://www.goarch.org/chapel/liturgical_texts/basil.

————. "Regulations, Greek Orthodox Archdiocese of America, 2019." Article IV, Section 5. https://www.goarch.org/documents/32058/3058354/2019+Regulations.pdf.

Gregory of Nazianzus. "Critique of Apollinarius and Apollinarianism." In *Nicene and Post-Nicene Fathers*, 2nd series, vol. 7, edited by Philip Schaff and Henry Wace, translated by Charles Gordon Browne and James Edward Swallow. Buffalo, NY: Christian Literature, 1894. Revised and edited for New Advent by Kevin Knight. http://www.newadvent.org/fathers/3103a.htm.

———. "Discourse 37." In *Nicene and Post-Nicene Fathers*, 2nd series, vol. 7, edited by Philip Schaff and Henry Wace, translated by Charles Gordon Browne and James Edward Swallow. Buffalo, NY: Christian Literature, 1894. Revised and edited for New Advent by Kevin Knight. http://www.newadvent.org/fathers/310237.htm.

Gregory of Nyssa. "On the Making of Man." In *Nicene and Post-Nicene Fathers*, 2nd series, vol. 5, edited by Philip Schaff and Henry Wace, translated by H. A. Wilson. Buffalo, NY: Christian Literature Publishing, 1893. Revised and edited for New Advent by Kevin Knight. http://www.newadvent.org/fathers/2914.htm.

Guroian, Vigen. "An Ethic of Marriage and Family." In *Incarnate Love: Essays in Orthodox Ethics*, 79–116. Notre Dame, IN: University of Notre Dame Press, 1987.

Hapgood, Isabel, trans. *Service Book of the Holy Orthodox-Catholic Apostolic Church*. Englewood, NJ: Antiochian Orthodox Christian Archdiocese, 1975.

Harvey, Susan Ashbrook. "Feminine Imagery for the Divine: The Holy Spirit, the Odes of Solomon, and Early Syriac Tradition." *St. Vladimir's Theological Quarterly* 37.2–3 (1993) 111–39.

Holy and Great Council. "Organization and Working Procedure of the Holy and Great Council of the Orthodox Church." Section 3.2. https://holycouncil.org/procedures.

Hopko, Thomas. "God and Gender: Articulating the Orthodox View." *St. Vladimir's Theological Quarterly* 37.2–3 (1993) 141–83.

———. "On the Male Character of the Christian Priesthood." In *Women and the Priesthood*, 97–134. 1st ed. Crestwood, NY: St. Vladimir's Seminary Press, 1983.

Howard, Agnes. *Showing: What Pregnancy Tell Us about Being Human*. Grand Rapids: Eerdmans, 2020.

Ignatius of Antioch. "Letter to Polycarp." In *The Apostolic Fathers*, vol. 2, edited and translated by Bart Ehrman, 310–21. Cambridge: Harvard University Press, 2005.

Irenaeus. "Against Heresies." Book V, Preface. In *Ante-Nicene Fathers*, vol. 1, translated by Alexander Roberts and William Rambaut, edited by Alexander Roberts et al. Buffalo, NY: Christian Literature, 1885. Revised and edited for New Advent by Kevin Knight. http://www.newadvent.org/fathers/0103500.htm.

Jansson, Laura S. *Fertile Ground: A Pilgrimage through Pregnancy*. Chesterton, IN: Ancient Faith, 2019.

John Chrysostom. "Homily 3 on Titus." In *Nicene and Post-Nicene Fathers*, 1st series, vol. 13, edited and translated by Philip Schaff. Buffalo, NY: Christian Literature, 1889. Revised and edited for New Advent by Kevin Knight. http://www.newadvent.org/fathers/23083.htm.

———. "Homily 12 on Colossians 4:18." In *On Marriage and Family Life*, translated by Catherine P. Roth and David Anderson, 73–80. Crestwood, NY: St. Vladimir's Seminary Press, 2003.

Kalkun, Andreas. "How to Ask Embarrassing Questions about Women's Religion: Menstruating Mother of God, Ritual Impurity, and Fieldwork among Seto Women in Estonia and Russia." In *Orthodox Christianity and Gender*, edited by Helen Kupari and Elina Voula, 97–114. London: Routledge, 2020.

Karras, Valerie A. "Eschatology." In *Cambridge Companion to Feminist Theology*, edited by Susan Parsons, 243–60. Cambridge: Cambridge University Press, 2002.

———. "Female Deacons in the Byzantine Church." *Church History* 73.2 (2004) 272–316.

———. "Patristic Views on the Ontology of Gender." In *Personhood: Orthodox Christianity and the Connection between Body, Mind, and Soul*, edited by John T. Chirban, 113–20. Westport, CT: Bergin & Garvey, 1996.

Kizenko, Nadieszda. "Feminized Patriarchy? Orthodoxy and Gender in Post-Soviet Russia." *Signs* 38.3 (2013) 595–621.

Kollontai, Pauline. "Contemporary Thinking on the Role and Ministry of Women in the Orthodox Church." *Journal of Contemporary Religion* 15 (2000) 165–79.

Kupari, Helen, and Elina Voula. *Orthodox Christianity and Gender*. London: Routledge, 2020.

Ladouceur, Paul. "The Ordination of Women to the Priesthood." In *Women and Ordination of the Orthodox Church: Explorations in Theology and Practice*, edited by Gabrielle Thomas and Elena Narinskaya, 166–86. Eugene, OR: Cascade, 2020.

———. Review of *Feminism and Tradition: Quiet Reflections on Ordination and Communion*. *St. Vladimir's Theological Quarterly* 60.3 (2016) 415–23.

Larin, Vassa. "What Is 'Ritual Im/purity' and Why?" *St. Vladimir's Theological Quarterly* 3.4 (2008) 284–85.

Louth, Andrew. Review of *That All Shall be Saved*. *Journal of Orthodox Christian Studies* 3.2 (2020) 235.

Linsley, Alice C. "Stepping into the Stream." *Road to Emmaus Journal* 11.1 (2010) 31–34.

Liveris, Leonie B. *Ancient Taboos and Gender Practice: Challenges for Orthodox Women and the Church*. Burlington, VT: Ashgate, 2005.

Madigan, Kevin, and Carolyn Osiek. *Ordained Women in the Early Church: A Documentary History*. Baltimore: Johns Hopkins University Press, 2005.

Merdjanova, Ina, ed. *Women and Religiosity in Orthodox Christianity*. New York: Fordham University Press, 2021.

Mitchell, Brian Patrick. *The Disappearing Deaconess: How the Hierarchical Ordering of Church Offices Doomed the Female Diaconate*. Alexandria, VA: Eremía, 2021.

# BIBLIOGRAPHY

Moran, Neil K. "Narthex of the Deaconesses in Hagia Sophia." https://orthodox deaconess.org/wp-content/uploads/2017/04/deaconesses-nmoran.pdf.

Morelli, George. "The Biopsychology of Sexuality and Orthodoxy: Some Reflections." In *Personhood: Orthodox Christianity and the Connection between Body, Mind and Soul*, edited by John T. Chirban, 107–19. Westport, CT: Bergin and Garvey, 1996.

Najim, Michel, and Patrick B. O'Grady, eds. "Service of Churching—of Woman and Child at Forty Days after Giving Birth." In *Services of Initiation into the Holy Orthodox-Catholic and Apostolic Church*, 17–31. LaVerne, CA: Antiochian Orthodox Institute, 2017.

Ngige, Ngorge John. "IOTA Missiology Seminary on Women's Ministries in Africa Webinar." November 2021.

Ochs, Vanessa L. *Inventing Jewish Ritual*. Philadelphia: Jewish Publication Society, 2007.

Orthodox Church in America. "Article III: The All-American Council." In *The Statute of the Orthodox Church in America*. https://www.oca.org/statute/article-iii.

———. "Service after Miscarriage or Stillbirth." https://www.oca.org/orthodoxy/prayers/service-after-a-miscarriage-or-stillbirth; or, https://www.oca.org/files/PDF/Music/Supplemental/service-after-miscarriage.pdf.

Peppard, Michael. "Household Names: Junia, Phoebe, & Prisca in Early Christian Rome." *Commonweal*, April 23, 2018. https://www.commonwealmagazine.org/household-names.

Pew Research Center. "The Gender Gap in Religion around the World." March 22, 2016. https://www.pewforum.org/2016/03/22/the-gender-gap-in-religion-around-the-world/.

"Prayers for a Woman on the Fortieth Day of Childbirth." In *The Great Book of Needs*, vol. 1, 10–11. South Canaan, PA: St. Tikhon's Seminary Press, 2000.

"Prayer for a Woman When She Has Miscarried/Aborted an Infant." In *The Great Book of Needs*, vol. 1, 16–18. South Canaan, PA: St. Tikhon's Seminary Press, 2000.

Protoevangelium of James. In *Ante-Nicene Fathers*, vol. 8, edited by Alexander Roberts et al., translated by Alexander Walker. Buffalo, NY: Christian Literature Publishing, 1886. Revised and edited for New Advent by Kevin Knight. http://www.newadvent.org/fathers/0847.htm.

Purpura, Ashley. "Constructing the Patriarchal Woman: Liturgical Challenges for Orthodox Christian Gender Equality." *Journal of Orthodox Christian Studies* 1.2 (2018) 167–88.

Pylvänäinen, Pauliina. *Agents in Liturgy, Charity and Communication: The Tasks of Female Deacons in the Apostolic Constitutions*. Turnhout: Brepols, 2020.

Regule, Teva. "An Interview with Metropolitan Kallistos Ware." *The St. Nina Quarterly* 1.3 (1997). http://www.stnina.org/print-journal/volume-1/volume-1-no-3-summer-1997/an-interview-bishop-kallistos-ware.

———. "Liturgy as Relationship: Reflections and Considerations on the Participation in the Liturgical Assembly of the Orthodox Church." Unpublished paper delivered at *Sophia Institute Conference*, 2008.

———. "The Role of Women in the Church: Is It Always about Ordination?" Unpublished paper delivered at *New Directions in Orthodox Christian Thought and Practice Conference*, 2017.

Roccas, Nicole. *Under the Laurel Tree: Grieving Infertility with Saints Joachim and Anna*. Chesterton, IN: Ancient Faith, 2019.

Russian Orthodox Church. *Basis of the Social Concept*. https://old.mospat.ru/en/documents/social-concepts/.

———. "On the Participation of the Faithful in the Eucharist: Document Approved at the Hierarchal Consultation of the Russian Orthodox Church, February 2–3, 2015 in the Cathedral of Christ the Saviour in Moscow." https://jordanville.org/files/Articles/On-the-Participation-of-the-Faithful-in-the-Eucharist-Edited.pdf.

———. "Unbaptized Infants Allowed Funeral Service in the Church." *Pravmir*, July 17, 2018. https://www.pravmir.com/unbaptized-infants-allowed-to-funeral-service-in-the-church/.

Saint Catherine's Vision. "A Call for the Rejuvenation of the Ministry of the Ordained Deaconess." http://saintcatherinesvision.com.

Schrodel, Jenny. *Naming the Child: Hope-filled Reflections on Miscarriage, Stillbirth, and Infant Death*. Brewster, MA: Paraclete, 2009.

Shaw, S. M. "Gracious Submission: Southern Baptist Fundamentalists and Women." *National Women's Studies Association* 20.1 (2008) 51–77.

St. Phoebe Center for the Deaconess. "Calls for the Rejuvenation of the Female Diaconate in the Modern Era." https://orthodoxdeaconess.org/wp-content/uploads/2021/02/Modern-Calls-For-Diaconate.pdf.

Streett, Matthew. "What to Do with the Baby? The Historical Development of the Rite of Churching." *St. Vladimir's Theological Quarterly* 56.1 (2012) 51–71.

Stuhlman, Byron David. *The Initiatory Process in the Byzantine Tradition*. Piscataway, NJ: Gorgias, 2009.

Synod of Antioch. "Announcement." *Word* magazine, September 1997, 33.

Taft, Robert F. "Women at Church in Byzantium: Where, When—and Why?" *Dumbarton Oaks Papers* 52 (1998) 27–87.

Theodorou, Evangelos. *'H Cheirotonia 'H Cheirothesia twn Diakoniswn*. Athens: Department of Theology, National and Kapodistrian University of Athens, 1954.

Theokritoff, Elizabeth. "Christ and Gender: Reviewing Konstantinos N. Yokarinis, *The Gender or Genderlessness of the Incarnate Christ* (Athens: Armos, 2011)." In *Women and Ordination of the Orthodox Church: Explorations in Theology and Practice*, edited by Gabrielle Thomas and Elena Narinskaya, 21–39. Eugene, OR: Cascade, 2020.

Thermos, Vasileios. "The Orthodox Church: Sexual Orientation, and Gender Identity: From Embarrassment to Calling." *The Wheel* 13.14 (2018) 83–90.

Thiani, Evangelos. "IOTA Missiology Seminary on Women's Ministries in Africa Webinar." November 2021.

Ukrainian Orthodox Church of the USA. *Initiation*. Forthcoming, 2023.

———. "XXXII Sobor." https://uocofusa.org.

U.S. Census Bureau. "American Community Survey, 2009–2013." https://www.census.gov/data/developers/updates/acs-5-yr-summary-available-2009-2013.html.

Vagaggaini, Cipriano. *Ordination of Women to the Diaconate in the Eastern Churches*. Collegeville, MN: Liturgical, 2013.

Vasiljević, Maxim. *Theology as Surprise: Patristic and Pastoral Insights*. Crestwood, NY: St. Vladimir's Seminary Press, 2018.

Vassiliadis, Petros. "Final Report of the International Scientific Symposium: Deaconesses, Past, Present, Future." https://www.academia.edu/41940677/FINAL_REPORT_OF_THE_INTERNATIONAL_SCIENTIFIC_SYMPOSIUM_Deaconesses_Past_-Present_-Future_Organization_Committee.

Ware, Kallistos. "Foreword." *The Wheel* 13.14 (2018) 6–10.

Wheeler, Rachel. *Desert Daughters and Desert Sons*. Collegeville, MN: Liturgical, 2020.

Wijngaards, John. *The Ordained Women Deacons of the Church's First Millennium*. Norwich, UK: Canterbury, 2012.

Wilson, Sarah Hinlicky. "Elizabeth Behr-Sigel's Trinitarian Case for the Ordination of Women." In *Women and Ordination of the Orthodox Church: Explorations in Theology and Practice*, edited by Gabrielle Thomas and Elena Narinskaya, 99–113. Eugene, OR: Cascade, 2020.

———. *Woman, Women, and the Priesthood in the Trinitarian Theology of Elisabeth Behr-Sigel*. London: T. & T. Clark, 2013.

Zagano, Phyllis. *Holy Saturday: An Argument for the Restoration of the Female Diaconate in the Catholic Church*. New York: Crossroad, 2000.

Zakarian, David. *Women, Too, Were Blessed: The Portrayal of Women in Early Christian Armenian Texts*. Leiden: Brill, 2021.

# Index

INDEX

Made in the USA
Las Vegas, NV
11 April 2023

70463615R00076